Stuck

Stuck

Maurizio Cattelan: The Unauthorized Autobiography

Francesco Bonami

Gagosian

I’ve always had trouble holding a pencil. Once, though, I did a great drawing of red mountains. Mom got mad. She said mountains were not red. She forced me to color them green. When I grew up, one day I was taking a walk at sundown, and I saw the mountains glowing red. And I thought: Mom was wrong.

—Maurizio Cattelan

FOREWORD

Are You Talking to Me?

This book is a myopic biopic of the life and art of Maurizio Cattelan, written by me, after listening to him for more than thirty years. Some events are semifictional, some are real, and some are pure imagination, based on what I have guessed Cattelan was thinking, feeling, or hiding. It is a book about an unlikely and unfinished friendship, about respect, lies, and truth. It is about communicating art, and the art of communication, about the skills of an artist that kills. This book is about an unforeseen chapter in the history of art in which a banana ended up inside a fountain—that is, Marcel Duchamp's urinal. You may choose to call him a prankster, a joker, a comedian, or a clown, but Cattelan has redefined the concept of being a "master." Here is my story of his story. You can believe it or not, it doesn't much matter. Just as long as you enjoy it, that's enough. If cultivating "doubt" is essential to life . . . well, Maurizio Cattelan harvests doubts like nobody else.

Introduction

To sleep perchance to scream? Too deep, perchance too stoned? Out of order? Out of luck? There's the rub . . . Sleep or lust? Sleeping or lost . . .

That's it, lost. Maurizio Cattelan has lived through the nightmare, rather than the dream, of being lost, of vanishing, being forgotten, winding up in the nowhere from whence he came.

Cattelan has lived with the terror of getting sucked down the drain of the washing machine that spewed dirty hot water into the basin in which, twice a week, as a kid, he had his bath. Fear of getting lost, of losing himself, of losing. A dreadful way to live for one of the Italian artists who has a rightful place in art history. They can never take that little corner away from him, that niche under the eaves that he has earned. In a few centuries from now, time will decide how many square feet he's going to get, but the minimum space essential to being considered one of the artists to have written a chapter in the long history of art, that has threatened to finish for millennia yet never does, is already guaranteed. In fact, he has conquered it, assertively, without asking anyone permission to do so.

So why is he so afraid of vanishing and getting lost? No one really knows. This book sets out to investigate every suspicion one might have about Cattelan. An unauthorized autobiography, written by yours truly over years and years of ongoing acquaintance and contact, here and there. Here is New York, there is Italy. A story that often fails to jibe because it skirts its way around things, avoiding the truth, though lingering on the threshold of the false. Cattelan is a contemporary Pinocchio and I'm like some poor Geppetto forced to listen to endless tall tales and half-truths in order to finally be able to gather the pitifully few serious, true things this artist manages to tell me.

Cattelan is a legend, not so much an urban legend as one rubbed out of a Neapolitan coffeepot. At first glance, nothing seems to have changed in his life, from his breakfast of bread soaked in *caffè latte* to his way of dressing—identical to the days when he scurried around the streets of Padua and then Forlì. But if we take a closer look, we see that everything has changed. This human marionette used to have nothing to lose, and no fear of getting lost. Today, now that he's a winner, now that he has cleaned up at the gaming table of luck, the things he does and says are nicely gauged, weighed up, measured, just in case someone might be listening, and might report on them, spill the beans or, in my case, tell the tale.

So my narrative is a yarn told by Cattelan to me in the hope that memory gaps can be filled with more dignified, frilly recollections. What you are about to read, is an autobiographical biography authored by the artist himself, but it is also a tale that feeds on hearsay and unchecked facts. What could be called "Cattelan's Conscience," as you have probably grasped, is based, with a total lack of humility, on *Zeno's Conscience* by Italo Svevo. It will thus be a work of biofiction—or as my poor uncle used to put it "biofarce"—in which truth and falsehood play ping-pong on the table of life—or that of one life: the life of Maurizio Cattelan. The net was set up on September 21, 2010, his fiftieth birthday—the same day his big middle finger, in a single stroke, sent all the crybabies and thieving ruffians of the *bel paese* to hell.

L.O.V.E. (2010) is the name of that finger, which some people say stands for Lions, Geese (*Oche*, in Italian), Vipers, and Elephants—namely the Italian zoo of our time and, it would seem, of the years to come. With that skyward pointing digit, it is as if Cattelan were some sort of contemporary Fra Cristoforo threatening the present with divine retribution. Cattelan is a Savonarola disguised as a street entertainer. Were it possible, the pope would excommunicate him, or rather, deprive him of the right to be a great communicator.

Cattelan has concocted his life on a desktop, or maybe a table in a bar, a sort of dinette-workshop: borrowing from Oliviero Toscani and Roberto Benigni to create a new version of himself. Just as Giorgio Morandi looked at his bottles long enough to make them become universal works of art, so Cattelan has stared so deeply at his own defects as to transform them into masterpieces. What I am about to tell is a true story: one part is serious, the other is wretched. Seriousness and wretchedness: the ingredients that have made this artist a genius of our time and who knows which others.

The Liar's Calling

One day I came home from school, and climbing the stairs at Via Ospedale Civile in Padua I saw my mother waiting for me at the door. She never waited for me like that. Actually, I was often the one waiting for her on the landing when she got back late from work. But this time she was standing there. Actually it was not my mom, but Signora Pierina Brillo who was waiting for Signor Maurizio Cattelan. Mom was inside. As soon as I came within reach she hauled me up and tried to whack me one, but I nimbly avoided the blow. "You broke the chair, you good-for-nothing!" she shouted. She didn't usually smack me or yell at me, but this time she did. Also because there were five of us in the house—me, my two sisters, and my parents—and we had exactly five chairs. If one of them was broken, somebody would have to eat standing up or sitting on the couch. "But I didn't break it," I answered. "Don't lie to me!" she yelled.

I really didn't break the chair, but she didn't believe me, and kept on asking me how it happened. I told her over and over that I hadn't done anything, that somebody else must have broken the chair, maybe one of my sisters, who was heavier than me.

The more I denied it, and the more I tried to find someone else to blame, the more furious she became. "Breaking a chair is already bad enough, but continuing to lie to me and accuse other people, that's just plain wretched!" I understood her viewpoint, but I didn't know what to do about it, since I hadn't done anything wrong. But the more I denied it the more Mom made it into a big deal. To try to make me confess, at a certain point she even started to cry, carrying on about one of her brothers who had died, I can't remember how, who had told so many lies that no one would give him a job anymore. She didn't want me to turn out like him, so she begged me to confess to the evil deed. I stood my ground, and though it wasn't easy—tears have never come easily to me—I was forced to start crying to make her believe me. For Mrs. Brillo, instead of proving my innocence, my tears were a sure sign of my guilt. "He doesn't just tell lies, he even cries about it! Scoundrel!" she yelled with all the anger she could muster. I sobbed and took the fifth, since I had no evidence, no proof, no alibi, though I really hadn't committed the crime. She wasn't about to change her mind. At a certain point, seeing no way out of the situation, I just decided to take the blame and put an end to it. "Yes Mom, I broke the chair. I stood on it and the leg bent; I tried to straighten it out and it broke off in my hand." Hearing that, Mom sat down limply on the shabby sofa and sighed, "So you've finally made up your mind to tell the truth . . . come over here." She pulled me to her and gave me a kiss of forgiveness, which I didn't deserve, since there was nothing to forgive.

It goes without saying that I was the one who had to eat dinner standing up. Later, in bed, under the covers, breath fogging the cold air, I had a sort of vision, or I heard a voice that came out of the wall and said: "Maurizio, from this day forth you will be a lifelong liar. Truth is more dangerous than falsehood." Ever since that day I have constructed most of my life around lies, climbing them as if they were ivy, covering them up to hide them from the world that was watching me.

On the Road to Vernasca

In Padua, the fog smells fishy. Once it descends and you can't see a thing, I have always smelled the stench of fish. It doesn't happen when it's sunny. My sisters said I was dumb, that fog has no smell, and Padua is not on the sea, so the stink I was talking about was all in my mind. Maybe there is a bad smell in my head. I almost never open the windows of my cranium because I am afraid that the few ideas I've got up there will fly away like parakeets that find the cage door open.

Anyway, when I woke up that day in my rented flat on Via Ugo Foscolo, outside the window the fog was thick and there was the usual fishy odor. Not the smell of the sea, mind you, but the smell of fish. I had left my last job, determined to never work again in my life. Or, more precisely, to never work for anyone except myself. Down in the street, wreathed in fog, like a horse awaiting its master, was my Motobi 125 Sport. I thought I heard it whinny. I've always been obsessed with horses, even though I have never been on one. The 125 Sport neighed because of the cold, or maybe to tell me to get up, go out, go somewhere, to give its poor carburetor a chance to breathe. I dipped a big slice of rustic bread into a cup of *caffè latte*, and when I pulled it out, dripping, I was already seated on the scooter, motor running, ready to go, wearing an orange windbreaker. I had no idea where I was going. The only thing I had decided was to go west, to get as far from the sea as possible, away from the stench of fish that had plagued me my whole life. The cod our mother made us eat with vegetable oil every damned blessed Friday.

I drove into the dense mist of the Po Valley plains—damp but at last aromatic. I crossed the border of Emilia Romagna and stopped for a mortadella sandwich. Back on the scooter the fog was lifting and the flat landscape was becoming visible. The road was empty, but as soon as I passed the sign for Vernasca the motor of the 125 let out a dreadful moan and stopped. The scooter stuttered. I put it in neutral and pushed it, running, for a few dozen meters. Then I quit. I tried to start it, but nothing happened. My horse was done for. I too collapsed by the road, with no idea how to fix the situation.

The sun started to warm things up a bit. Every so often, a truck or a car went by. I thought about the art exhibition I had seen in Padua. I knew nothing, but what came to mind in just that moment, with almost no lire in my pocket and a dead scooter, were the works of an artist called Pistoletto. Mirrors with figures and objects. I remember seeing myself reflected in one panel, an unwitting and temporary character in an artwork, and it made an impression on me. It was hard to recall if the sensation was one of pleasure or curiosity. Anyway, lying there with nothing to do, nothing to hope for, nothing to look at made me decide that maybe art could become a job—the job that would give me the chance to work only for myself.

The only art I knew about was what I had found in an art history book by Giulio Carlo Argan, which I had bought second-hand after seeing the mirror exhibition. No one ever talked about art at home. The only music we listened to was on the radio, which played from morning to night, even when the house was empty. My mother said it would discourage burglars. But no burglars would ever have targeted our building. If anything, they lived there. Had they shown up, the only thing of value they might have stolen was precisely that radio.

So art was not part of my vocabulary. And yet now, sitting by the road, something inside me had stimulated my appetite for it. I closed my eyes and thought about what it would be like to feel like an artist. I thought maybe musicians understand they are musicians because inside them they can hear music playing, like the radio in our house. But an artist? What can a person who has to make things hear inside? To be an artist, I thought, maybe you have to be able to see things inside you that don't exist elsewhere. But that didn't work, because the mirrors I had seen, with my image reflected in them, had certainly not been invented by that chap there. So what had that guy done, anyway? How had he become an artist? I just couldn't understand it. But the less I understood it, the more I wanted to be an artist. Did people become artists just like that, in one stroke, without even knowing it? Your scooter breaks down and you realize you have to be an artist.

I wondered how the mirror guy had figured out that he was an artist. If I had had his phone number I would have called him from the first payphone and asked: "Sorry, but could you tell me exactly when you decided to be an artist, or to make art?" Because actually, I was also wondering something else: Do you become an artist, or are you simply an artist? The becoming option—that one chooses to be an artist—was better for my purposes because I definitely didn't feel like an artist. The only artistic thing I had ever done was to use a marker to put mustaches on little statues of St. Anthony at the church where I was an altar boy on Sundays. When the pastor found out, he sent me home and didn't allow me to be an altar boy anymore. That was the first time in my life that I got fired. At home I got the silent treatment that evening at dinner. I think that deep inside, my parents, Pierina and Paolo, sort of hoped I would become a priest, go to the seminary, and get rid of all their worries. My mother hoped I had a vocation. My expulsion from the parish sent all their dreams up in smoke. Well, maybe being an artist is a bit like becoming a priest or a monk. You have to have a vocation. So I was in trouble, because there on the ground on the road to Vernasca, I didn't feel any calling. Anything but St. Paul, I'm St. Peabrain, I said to myself. Even so, the image of my face peering out from behind the shoulders of the two black and white figures on the mirror kept returning to my mind. I had been a work of art, but I couldn't be an artist.

I was sitting there pondering these things when I heard a female voice with a Romagnolo accent from the window of a Fiat 500: "Are you OK? Did you hurt yourself?" A young woman was worried about me. She thought I might have had an accident. Her name was Fabrizia. She offered to give me a lift, and since I didn't really know where I was going she took me with her to Forlì.

I Should Not Have Existed

Actually, I should never have even existed. My parents were expecting a girl, and when I was born they were very disappointed. I already had an adult nose, I looked deformed. I wasn't supposed to exist. My parents even forgot to register my birth at the town hall, on September 21, 1960. They didn't even give me a name. The *carabinieri*, who came the next day on the feast day of San Maurizio, reminded them that it was obligatory to give a name and register the birth of one's children. I've always had the suspicion that they were considering leaving me somewhere in a crate. But some people, like my uncle, for instance, said that just the opposite happened—that my parents found me in a crate and took me in. Crate or fate, more or less the same thing. But I've always had the sensation of being a kid who was left in a crate somewhere. A state of mind that has always made me feel like a recovered, recycled individual, who has never really been new.

Every summer they would send me to camp. I got on the bus and when it drove off the sound of the motor was like the sigh of relief my mother heaved, to finally be free of this shyly dangerous and treacherous creature. I stayed at camp for a few weeks, then went home without ever knowing what home would be. I could have found an empty house. Once, at the bus stop, where parents were picking up their kids after vacation, I was left there by myself, with the bus driver, who didn't know what was to be done or what to do with me. We waited a while until it was clear that no one was coming to get me. The driver told me to get back on the bus, and he took me home, like in a taxi: I was happy as a clam. When my mother opened the door and saw me with the driver she asked me what I was doing there. She had made a mistake with the dates, she told me: She thought I was coming home the next day. I have never really believed that. I've always thought she was hoping I'd never return. Not because she wasn't fond of me—she loved me a lot. It was because she had thought, from the start, that my fate lay elsewhere. She didn't want my life to turn out like hers, made of the remains of the day that society allowed her. Her hugs were like little thrusts, pushing me away from her even as she caressed me.

My father was like an empty refrigerator: quite cold and essential. He worked all day as a truck driver, but when he came home he was a vivid presence, like an appliance. You could always understand what his purpose was. He was our Dad, no more and no less. Just as nobody can think a refrigerator is a kerosene heater, we never thought that our father could be something different from what we saw. It never entered our minds to ask him for something more than what he was, than what he gave us, what he represented. He was perfectly aware of the limits of his dignity, and this enabled him to never complain, never have regrets or insatiable desires. So we too never asked for anything more than what was around us. I don't think I ever expressed a wish for something I didn't have and others had. Were we unhappy? I don't think so. We made do with the state of mind we had, without too much pretension. I might say that we were a subproletarian Zen family—in the sense that we were never resigned to our economic and social condition.

One day, when I was quite a few years older, I went on a trip to Armenia. Well, that country reminds me of our family. If I had to say what my family was like, I'd say it was like Armenia. How so? In the sense that Armenia is a country where there is almost nothing, yet there is everything. An everything that cannot be seen, but can be felt. At home, thinking back, there was everything, even if you couldn't see it. A nothing full of everything. I never heard anyone say, and I never uttered, the phrase "I wish I could . . ." We knew, and I have always known since then, that you can be satisfied with what you have—that real pleasure comes only from what we are capable of having, no matter what it is, or how much. Wishful thinking is a curse, it makes you permanently dissatisfied, full of regrets and envy. The only regret I think I sensed in our house was the invisible one of my mother on my account. She wanted me to deserve more, but she lived with the hidden fear that I would never be able to deserve anything, or at least anything better. When I banked the money from my first sold artwork I could almost feel one of her caresses. But this time it was not a push, but a real hug that brought me closer to her, even though she had already been dead for many years.

Even the affection we felt in our family was a subproletarian Zen affection. We consumed feelings cautiously, like the kerosene for the heater and the hot water discharged by the washing machine, which we used twice a week to take a bath in a washbasin. We loved each other just enough for it to be understood. We couldn't waste energy on emotions—energy that might come in handy later in adult life.

Work Makes You Tired

Even today, whatever I'm doing, I say I am "working." As if I feel guilty about not doing any real labor. Actually I've been working since I was sixteen. I've done jobs of all kinds. But not the "all kinds" of the adventurer. Just work of all types, to try to live better than the way I had learned to live. I've never been scared of work, but I never really wanted to do it either. Maybe that is why today I say I am working, when instead I'm just having fun. Not because I feel guilty, but because I am terrified at the thought of being unemployed. For me, being unemployed amounts to a state of weakness and destitution. The idea of being unemployed still frightens me. When I can't find an idea for my work—which is art—I feel like I am back in Padua, where I would really try to get a job and often fail to find one. Or maybe I would find work, only to lose it after a few weeks.

It is hard to explain the sensation of being unemployed to someone who has never experienced it. It's like having a wall in front of you: a sense of claustrophobia that fills you with the terror of getting closed up inside poverty. Suffocated by abjection forever. As long as I lived at home I didn't understand anything about poverty or work. I made do with what I had. But when I moved away from home, at the age of sixteen, I started to understand that it is possible to lack all kinds of things, and that to get them you have to work, and if you don't work you have to steal them. But you will never be able to steal peace of mind. When I was out of work I stole things, but I never managed to get back that subproletarian Zen state of mind my parents had always had. I did lots of different jobs, but today they all seem the same.

My last job was as a nurse. I didn't mind working with other people's bodies—even dead ones, like the time they punished me by sending me to wash corpses at the morgue. That was where I became aware of my own body. Only when you are next to a dead body and touch it can you realize the difference between being dead and alive. If you never try it, you never catch on. Or at least I had never caught on. Perhaps this is why my body is so important for my art now. I always try to imagine what my corpse might be like. I would love to be able to see it, the way I looked at the cadavers of others.

When my mother died, I quit working. I don't know why, I just did. I'm not sure it really had anything to do with my mother's death. But loss is always also a form of freedom. This time it was her moving away from me. I thought that the fate towards which she had been pushing me for so long was finally starting. Suddenly, I no longer wanted to work to support myself. My life was already a hard enough job. Moreover, you cannot be made unemployed by life. Life is a full-time job. My mother had fired life, not vice versa.

I tried to imagine how it works when you die. And since nothing came to mind and it frightened me to think about that moment, I imagined it being exactly like work. But in this case, you are the personnel manager. I imagined my mother calling her life into her office and saying: "Listen, starting tomorrow we no longer require your services." This idea of summoning your life and giving it a pink slip cheered me up. To think that life depends on us, not the opposite, was reassuring. Looking at life as a job made life and all its decisions easier for me. The first decision was to quit working.

The Devil's Building

Fabrizia was sexy as hell at the wheel of her 500. She asked me what I did before she asked my name. I thought that was weird enough—someone who cares more about what you do than who you are. "I'm an artist," I answered. And she turned to look at me, I can't remember if it was with amazement or suspicion. I had decided to be an artist, there, beside the road, thinking about that guy's mirrors. Fabrizia was my first chance to see if I could state my new profession. It just popped out of my mouth—"I'm an artist"—and I didn't even know what it meant.

Things got problematic when after the amazement or suspicion, Fabrizia asked me what kind of art I made. Paintings? Sculpture? She had caught me off guard. "I make useless objects," I replied. She didn't get it and asked me to give her an example. I said I didn't like to tell people about my ideas, that I was afraid they'd steal them and make the artwork in my place. Fabrizia called me an idiot more than once and said she couldn't care less about my ideas and my art. She said she had other things on her mind. I figured she was talking about sex, but I was so shy when it came to such things that I made out that I didn't understand. In the end, Fabrizia kept on questioning me so I had to come up with something. I told her the last thing I'd made was an old hat I had transformed into a pot by attaching the handle of a real pot. Fabrizia was really enthusiastic about this sculpture of mine; she said it was really cool, that I would have lots of success, and that one day I would have to show her that pot-hat.

I don't know if that was the moment, maybe it wasn't, but it definitely came shortly after: I thought I would like to invent things that are usually useful for something, but then wind up serving another purpose. Not even I really understood what I was thinking, but it seemed like a good first step in my career as an artist. In fact, then and there, I decided to hire myself out as an artist. It would be my new job. Then I asked Fabrizia where we were headed. Forlì, she said. She lived there. I'd never been there.

Fabrizia lived in a place known as the Devil's Building. I had wound up there, already in hell, without having done anything wrong.

Forlì Is Not New York

I could say that Forlì put me under a spell. I had just decided to be an artist and there I was, having to prove it. In Forlì. Proving you are an artist in Forlì is not as hard as doing it in New York, but it isn't all that simple either. In the Italian provinces, "artist" is a synonym for "dunce." And in fact everyone looked at me as if I were stupid. The person who looked at me the most like a dunce was a photographer who did portraits and weddings. I would go to his shop every day, without fail, to get him to photograph what I thought might be art but actually was not, never has been, and never will be, even though today, some people would like to believe that what I did back then had to be, must be, should be art.

The trouble is, to make art, it is not enough to be an artist. I didn't know that when I was in Forlì. I rode around on my bicycle all day, without imagining that I would make art for my whole life. It is no coincidence that my first sculptures were assembled bicycle frames. I thought they were just great. Even today I think they are great. But they seemed even better when, one day, I entered a well-known gallery in New York and found a sculpture by a famous artist made just like my bicycles. I felt both honored and sad. Really sad to have been so close to art and not taken advantage of it—in Forlì, not in New York. But I had already learned that before making art you have to find it, maybe steal it, never copy it. Picasso was right. Only the competent copy. Geniuses and failures steal. I added the failures because it'll come in handy, but also because I think it's true. The failed artist is closer to the genius than the good artist. The good artist understands everything and tries to do the best thing that comes into his or her head. The genius and the failure understand nothing, absolutely nothing. They just do it. Still, not knowing I was a genius, I did it. I did, did, did.

But one day I got tired of doing. I was tired of the Devil's Building, tired of Forlì, its streets. I got tired of the wedding photographer. I felt the urgency to feel good, to be good. I decided on the day and the time. As I had already done before on my 125 Sport, and before that on my Califfo moped, I decided to set off for Barcelona. No matter what the weather, I would leave. But this time I was a pauper. No more 125, no more Califfo. Just my bicycle—the only one I hadn't turned into a sculpture.

Seven in the morning on the appointed day. A hurricane outside. I ate my usual breakfast with the usual slice of bread, the usual cup of *caffè latte*. I looked at the yellow formica kitchen table. My girlfriend had damaged it with a hot iron. I had fixed it by taking out the hole and joining the two halves. It was really small now. It was depressing. Everything was depressing. I made myself sad. The only thing that wasn't depressing was my bike, waiting for me outside like a faithful dog. Even if I had found it as a stray, abandoned on a street corner.

I put on my hooded rain cape and went outside. The bike was looking at me from the other side of the street, chained to a lamppost. I looked back. The rain was pouring down. It must have been a Tuesday. It must have been eight in the morning.

At noon I was still out in the rain, on the Adriatic state highway, pedaling. Every time a truck passed it drenched me with water and made me swerve. But I forged on. At 1:30pm I stopped for a bite to eat. The rain kept on. I kept on pedaling. I arrived someplace. The rain was over. The air was squeaky clean. The sea was choppy. The sun had come out.

I remember that just like the time I was sitting by the road with my broken-down scooter, I thought again about the artist with the mirrors. Then I thought about a horrid fiberglass cactus that was supposed to be a fountain, called *Adelina's Anxiety*, I had shown in my first exhibition, in a bar in Bologna. I don't remember who Adelina was, but I remember the anxiety, which was my own. For the first time in my life as an artist, I felt a sense of shame. I would later feel ashamed many times when looking at one of my works that had ended up in a museum or maybe the home of some collector.

Bad ideas have a more enticing voice than good ones. It is easier to listen to them. But when you go to bed with them, you can never break free. I imagined one of those mirrors, and together with the figures seen from behind, there I was, in black and white, bare chested, looking back at myself with scorn. It started to get dark. The steam from my soaked clothing entered my nostrils. I sneezed violently. After that I spent a week in bed with a high fever. When I next saw the sun, I was in Milan.

Intelligent Design

Nobody. I knew nobody in Milan at the end of the 1980s. I had "found" a bicycle as usual and I rode around the city like a poor jerk. Art, I thought, is bigger than I am. Being an artist, I reasoned, was a job I took without a contract, and now I didn't know how to resign from it. At the time, the hottest thing in Milan was "design." My cactus-fountain in Bologna was really design. Or at least the Bolognese critics who had seen it thought so.

I remember seeing my image reflected in the window of a design store in Milan. The window did something similar to the mirrors by that artist, whose first and last name I now knew: Michelangelo Pistoletto. They told me that I too could be part of this world of created and creative things and knickknacks. I looked at myself in the glass and it seemed like I was inside the store, in the midst of all those objects, furniture, sofas, tables, lamps, chairs. Those objects looked simple enough to think up and make. Then I saw the light. I had become an artist, and there was no need to resign from my job. I could just transfer to a new department. I remain an artist, but I become a designer, which for me was more or less the same thing.

The problem wasn't art, the problem was ideas, and it seemed easier to get an idea for a seat or a table than for a sculpture or a painting. I had always been around tables and chairs. I knew how tables talked and how chairs kept quiet. It was much harder to listen to a painting. Very hard indeed.

In the end, when I had removed the hole made by the hot iron on the formica table I had done a design operation. Though the most designer type thing I had seen was precisely the form of the iron that had made the hole. So my first creation as a designer was a series of placemats with the form of an imprint from an iron. Six burned imprints on which to set dishes. An American-style table service. I gave it a title: *Sergio*. What did that have to do with anything? Well, my girlfriend had cheated on me with a guy called Sergio. When she forgot the iron on the table in our kitchen, I think it was because she was dreaming about him.

I produced *Sergio* myself. I bought plastic and an iron and I left the hot iron on the plastic until it burned and the brand remained. I repeated the operation six times.

I returned to the store that had given me the idea. I went in and found the owner. He was affable enough, a little strange, but willing to listen. He ended up listening to me for the rest of his life, because from that day on, that gentleman became my manager, agent, and friend—the ideal spectator with whom I would test every artwork, every title, every dumbass idea that came into my head. As luck would have it, he too was named Sergio. He liked the idea, but thought the production was terrible, so he proposed doing a prototype. "Where do you live?" he asked me. "No place," I replied. "If you like, when the store is closed you can sleep in here." He showed me a storeroom with a window, full of sofas and beds. I chose the most comfortable of the lot. I lived in that store for one year. I kept on designing objects. Some of them, to my amazement, even sold. Others just sat there. I had become the company's designer. Alongside the more conventional and commercial things something more creative was needed. Milan was all creativity in those years, and if you didn't give the impression of wanting to make something fun, light, humorous, brilliant, no one paid any attention to you.

Then at a certain point people stopped buying things in our store, and Sergio had to close. That was a big relief, because

I had understood that I was no designer, or at least if I were, I was finding it boring. I had gone back to flirting with art and things seemed to be coming out better than before. Society was changing around me. The magnificent 1980s were over. I was becoming more middle class. Middle-class girlfriends, middle-class friend-friends, middle-class needs, like a house to live in. *Mamma mia*, I thought at a certain point: If I keep it up, I'll end up tying the knot. If I get married, that's the end of everything.

I didn't marry, but I did make my first real work of art. It was about love, but at the same time it told love to go fuck itself. That bourgeois love, made of hypocrisy and little rules to be broken whenever necessary. Like holding hands—the signal in code to tell the others, the loners, the losers, the widows and widowers: "Look how much we're in love . . . the two of us." This physical, public, artificial union, with the illusion and hope that thoughts would also go hand in hand, along with desires. I wasn't cut out for that kind of love. Girls left me or I left them because I didn't want to hold hands. I needed my hands to carry my bicycle, my true companion from which I could not be separated. Without the bike I felt really alone, truly disarmed. The bicycle was the best escape route from a relationship, an argument, a discussion. As soon as things went sour, I was already on the bike and pedaling for all I was worth, never looking back, deaf to insults, shouts, and sobs. Girls hated the fact that I showed up on dates with my bike. They always asked me to park it someplace, and I would invent all kinds of excuses to avoid the separation. Once, one of my girlfriends managed to chain the bicycle to a pole and steal the key, which she returned to me only the next morning. In short, the bike was my way of defying familiar, intimate, bourgeois conventions.

This is why the first work of art I made was called *Lessico familiare* (*Family Syntax*). That was in 1989. The Berlin Wall had been knocked down the previous evening. I stripped, and a friend of mine took a photograph of me holding my hands

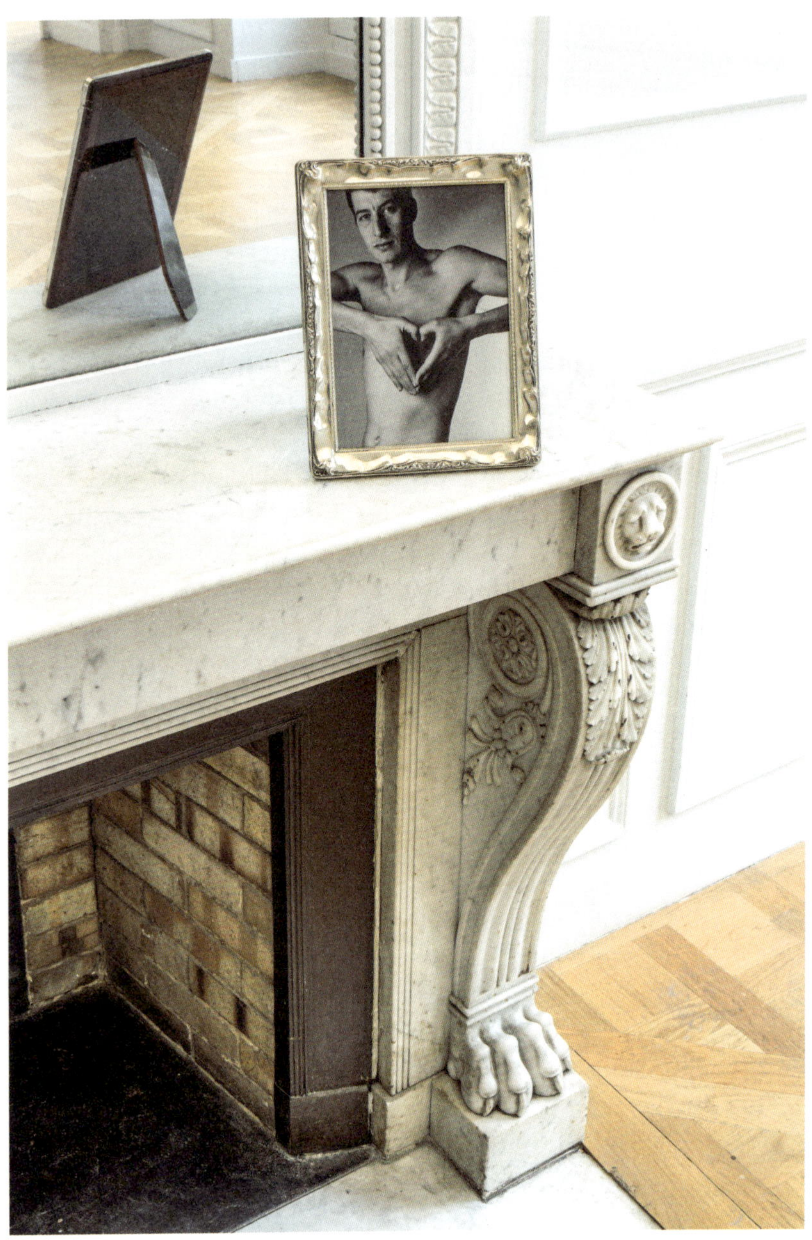

Installation view, *Lessico familiare* (1989) in *Not Afraid of Love*, Monnaie de Paris, 2016

in front of my chest, imitating the form of a heart. Then one day, I went to one of my girlfriends' parents' homes and saw an empty silver frame on a cabinet—one of those things people get as a wedding present. I stuck it in my bag and took it home. When I got back I inserted the black and white photo of me with my hands making a heart.

That was my first work of art. It was so simple. So immediate. So banal. It was 100% me—as I could never be again. The wall that divided my identity in two had been knocked down. On one side, the free loser, on the other, the artist who would be chained to his ambitions from that moment on. Two Cattelans became one inside that silver frame. The silver frame was art, or the conventions of art, and I had put myself in there. I would always be trapped inside that frame. Two souls had become one. But I have always missed that twin who lived inside me, that second, wiser Cattelan who was hidden in my gut. As an artist, I would always talk to him. That mini-me which would later also become one of my sculptures.

Election Campaign

Forget being an artist, I should have been a mayor. Not of a big city, but a small town, with just a few people. Those places where the mayor is also the confessor and psychoanalyst of the residents. A do-it-all mayor.

I was already an artist when this idea of also being something of a politician began to whet my appetite. I didn't have one thin dime, never mind the wherewithal for an election campaign. I hung out in Milan and Bologna with the petty cash I'd get now and then from the tables and chairs I had designed. When funds ran low I'd call on Sergio, the guy from the furniture store, and he would help me out with a few lire. The art world at the end of the 1980s was still wasted from the Transavanguardia binge. Most artists were still making paintings in the hope of getting famous like Sandro Chia, Francesco Clemente, and Enzo Cucchi. Since I didn't even know how to hold a pencil, I felt like I was automatically excluded from having any financial success.

In the meantime, Italy was bursting with affluence. The socialists were still holding court on all fronts. In Milan, in a gallery on Via Cusani, I remember seeing an exhibition by a Florentine painter—dreadful stuff, but it all sold. I saw him in one corner of the gallery, all puffed up, clearly feeling like Picasso himself. This triggered a special hatred in me and an aversion to everyone who painted. I could never have imagined that one day, I would meet that irritating painter again, outside my building in New York, and that we would become the best of friends. He had stopped being an artist and worked as a veterinarian in a clinic in the East Village. He helped me a lot with my works with animals. Every so often he would give me some dog that had had to be put to sleep, whose owners couldn't afford a burial. I would take care of the funeral rites. It made me a little money, and I also got some ideas for sculptures.

During that period in Milan and Bologna, New York did not exist in my head. The biggest journey I made back then was the long trip home at night after roaming around all day doing who remembers what. I hung around and we talked about everything. Politics was always there, in the newspapers, on TV. We felt left out, even if we had firm, radical views. The Red Brigades had lost their sheen, a bit like Arte Povera in those years—a dusty, nostalgic movement that dreamed of a revolution that was clearly never going to happen.

One evening I went to dinner at the home of a well-off young woman with artistic ambitions. We smoked all we could smoke and drank all we could drink. The next morning I woke up in the girl's bed, with no idea how I had got there. She seemed to know more about it than I did. I don't remember if she was attractive, only that she was pleasingly plump. Over breakfast she told me that if I wanted, she would help me to make a work of art. I told her the next work was going to be an advertisement in a newspaper urging people not to vote. One week later, in the local section of the newspaper, next to a photograph of the leader of the Socialist Party, Bettino Craxi, my advertisement appeared with the slogan, "Your vote is precious. HANG ONTO IT."

Love and politics have always come to blows inside my head, and what's worse is they have never worked together in my art. But I have always made use of them to better understand the world around me. Anyone who says I am a political artist is talking nonsense. In the sense that I have never been an "engaged" artist. Actually, I have always tried to disengage myself from everything, in both personal and public relationships. The only commitment I've taken seriously was that of getting myself as far away from poverty as possible, even though the void from which I came was, and still is, hot on my trail, and I can feel it breathing down the back of my neck. For me, politics is like a piece of modeling clay for a sculptor. I use it to make something else, to say something of a different nature. I treat politics like pottery, just as I roast human emotions: When they come out of the kiln they should be unrecognizable, though maybe they are more fragile than they were before.

The fragility of my ideas has always been a problem for me. If there is just one crack in what comes to mind I throw the whole thing out. People asked me if my newspaper advertisement was meant to urge people not to vote. I didn't know what to say because I hadn't even thought about abstention. Actually, I had no political message. My utterly flawed idea was that a vote is a private, personal thing, so it is very precious. If you give away your vote to someone else, you no longer have it. We shouldn't waste the few precious things that no one can ever truly take away from us, like our opinions, our innermost ideas, our fears. Voting, for me, meant giving others the right to govern our freedom of thought. When I tried to explain these things I got treated like an idiot, off and on. Even the girl who had paid for the newspaper ad was disappointed. She thought she had gotten her hands on a leader, and instead she realized I was just a naïve joker. We stopped seeing each other. I had lost my first supporter. I had to go back to the drawing board and start all over again.

Time Is Late

If you were not born an artist but decide to be one, time seems to drag on endlessly. Like there's no tomorrow. On an artist's calendar there are no numbers and names of months, just the same word, over and over: today. One today after another. Today, today, today, today: 365 todays a year, 7 todays a week. You feel like those models of ships trapped in bottles. I even made an artwork about this sensation of time that is always running late and never changes. It was called *Grammatica quotidiana* (*Everyday Grammar*) (1989): a real calendar with the name of a bakery in Forlì that financed the operation. I was becoming a "homemade artist." Homemade, mind you, not homespun. My art has always been very orderly, never coarse, never lumpy "but tasty." If anything, it is smooth and mean.

It would have been nice if someone, talking about what I did, had written a theory of "homemadeness"—the homemade aesthetic. A very particular aesthetic where industry succumbs to domestic necessity. Where the machine stoops to the banality of the dinette. Where mechanics accept the compromise of handiwork.

Those were the characteristics of my art. Not made by hand, but invented at home. Never in the studio. I have never had a studio. I have never had an assistant or a secretary. I am a "single father" artist, in the sense that my works never have a mom. The moms of my works have always abandoned them and left them to be raised by their dad. As the singer, Enzo

Jannacci would have said: "I am a single art father, begging to make ends meet, I am a sinner for this society . . ."

Yes, a sinner for the society that populates the world of art. I have never been officially baptized by the "militant critics," who have always seen me as a fraud on two legs; the maker of art that makes you laugh and then, like jokes, is immediately forgotten. A mortal sin for which there can be no absolution. Every one of my works is a useless act of contrition in search of a salvation I will never be granted. I am condemned to the moment, the today that munches on yesterday to placate the hunger of tomorrow. I am standing by the art tracks, but art doesn't stop at this station. If I get on that train, I have to do it like a stowaway, without a ticket, avoiding trouble by making the conductor laugh. But he also makes me get off at the next station.

Made in a Day

As Clint Eastwood said when he was Dirty Harry: "Make my day." Which in my case translates to: made in a day. Ever since I was a kid, I have had the sensation of having lost a day. Maybe it's because they registered my birth one day late, depriving me of twenty-four hours. In any case, I constantly worry that I might need one more day. Even with my first shows, I always found myself there one day before the opening, still without work to display, because I always needed one more blessed day. For a show in Bologna, on the day of the opening I put a sign on the door that said "Be right back." When the gallery owner arrived he got really angry. And he was even madder when he entered the space and found it empty—no works at all. I was AWOL. When I came back the gallery was still empty, but the "Be right back" sign had become a work hanging on the wall.

I've always liked this "be right back" idea, without saying when it was that someone left. The "right" is relative to the reader, not the writer of the message. You can never know just how long that "right" has become. A way to keep people still, waiting, available. A test to figure out if they really need you "right away." Because if they really need you right away, they will also wait quite a while. If they are not actually in a hurry to get you, they'll leave and come back some other time.

I also considered getting back my lost day by stealing the time from others, making them wait as long as possible. It's cruel, but that's the way it is. Lost time can be picked from the pockets of others. Something like umbrellas that get lost or somebody steals from you. Or bicycles. If they steal one from you, you have the right to steal another. At least I've always thought things worked something like that. You're just not supposed to steal a bicycle if yours hasn't been stolen. That would upset the whole thievery ecosystem. Theft should not be accumulation, but the filling of an existing void.

The same is true of art. If you want to steal an idea from somewhere, you can do it only when one of your ideas has been used by somebody else before you got a chance. I've always wondered if the second painter in the history of art to paint a crucifixion copied or stole the idea from the first one. Who knows if this anonymous first painter got mad when he saw the other picture with the same subject. Maybe not. Maybe it was a healthier environment, where the real challenge was to do the same thing, to work on the same idea and the same subject, and do it better than the others. Which is what happens today with shoes.

No shoemaker tells another shoemaker that he stole the idea of the shoe. The important thing is to make a better looking, more comfortable, sturdier, nicer shoe. That's what it must have been like with the crucifixions and depositions. A contest to see who could do the most effective, most interesting, most profound version. The cursed notion of the unique new idea is a fixation of just the last couple of centuries. I think copyright was invented by somebody who didn't have many ideas, so as to protect them by law. Instead, I agree with the ancients. There are not so many things out there to represent, and you can't buy the rights to them. The winner is the one who represents the world in the best way, at the right moment, with the most clarity or depth. It depends on taste.

Art is like telling a beautiful love story. The juice of it is always the same, but it depends how you pour it and then drink it—that's what makes it beautiful or not. As I said, I have a rather strange idea of love. I prefer not to fall in love, though when it has happened there hasn't been much I could do about it. Today, though, I do something about it, because if you fall in love, you end up losing those days you gained through such hard work. Days spent on love are days that can never come back, because love, no matter what they say about it, is always destined to end, to get to the dregs, and when it is gone you look back and you realize you have lost days, months, years. "Make me make back a day": that's what Dirty Harry should have said. I say it when I see a woman I like. It is a spell, a prayer, as if to say "Keep your distance, don't steal the time I'm always lacking." Instead of saying "I love you," I say, "Be right back." It's my curse. To run away from everything and everyone, in pursuit of that lost day.

In Search of the Lost Day

My little madeleine, like that of Proust, that brought the most distant memories to mind, the sweetest moments, an indolence so strong as to take the place of any other sentiment—well, my little madeleine is a slice of homemade bread with a thin coat of margarine, dipped in *caffè latte*. This slice of bread and margarine, every time it enters my mouth in the morning, plunges me into primal reveries. That taste is so strong that it can overcome any other flavor or odor. I remember that when I was a kid I would cram it all into my little mouth, getting drips all over me, and I could forget about the stink of the cabbage soup my mother was already cooking for dinner. I could forget the sharp odor of the skin of my two little sisters, the smell of my father, and that of my mother's quilted dressing gown. My slice of bread. They don't make 'em like that anymore.

Today I've moved on to butter, but that's hypocrisy. I would still like to eat margarine, slightly stale bread, and the long-life milk that made us feel almost rich back then because it was something new. Today the bread is dipped in semi-skimmed milk. My life has been skimmed too—it's healthier, but in the end it's a bit less rich than before. Less rich in sensations that were once so basic that there was no need to explain them, or even to think about them. "From Margarine to Butter"—that might be a good title for my autobiography. Milk no longer makes that layer of cream I hated so much as a kid. I don't know why. And nor does milk today make that horrid skin when you heat it up. I looked at the cup with that skin on top, and the fog outside the window pressing coldly against the glass, and I wanted to cry but I couldn't. I've never really been able to cry. I think it might be a question of anatomy, not of emotions. I was born without an excess of tears—just enough to moisten my corneas.

Tears and Rice

I can still recall my mother's tears, as she stood over a pot full of rice, the day they brought me home from the parish center after I had used a marker to draw a black mustache on the statue of St. Anthony. The pastor didn't even ask who had done it—he headed straight for me, whacked me, and sent me home. That was the end of my career as an altar boy. My mother really wanted me to be an altar boy. She was afraid I might become a communist. I was standing there by the door and she was crying silently over the rice. The rice we would have to eat for dinner. I still remember that I didn't care that my mother was crying, but I was grossed out by the idea of tears in my food.

That evening, at dinner, my father appeared grim about my misadventures, my mother was sad, and my sisters wouldn't stop gabbing. To manage to swallow one spoonful of rice I had to guzzle a whole glass of water, because I wanted to throw up at the idea of eating Mom's tears.

Eat your tears. Not a bad turn of phrase, actually. Instead of eating your words, eat your tears. Regret your pain and your troubles. In any case, I ate the rice, I ate the sobs on the plate, and I went to bed with undigested tears in my gut.

Forced to Be Illicit

After so many years in the art world I still have the sensation of being an illicit intruder. Of operating without an art license. There is always the danger that someone will come along and take my place, kick me out, or write me a ticket for occupation of art space without a permit. It is not a pleasant feeling. But it's also my fault. I've always introduced myself as a squatter. At an art fair in Bologna I occupied a corner with a little table where I gathered funds for my soccer team, *A.C. Forniture Sud* (1991). It was a team composed of African immigrants. I will admit, however, that I was an early disrupter, illegal ahead of the times. Twenty years ago you didn't hear all this talk about immigration, there were not frequent boats arriving on Lampedusa. There was no Umberto Bossi to say "*Fora da i ball*" (northern Italian dialect for "piss off"). But I was there, and I gave my team an imaginary sponsor called Rauss, which in German means the same thing: "Get out." I was the coach, and I got my team into matches. But it was always chaos, a fracas. My little table to raise funds for the team might have been illicit, but it was intriguing. It was an official way of being illicit. I felt like the head of a real soccer team. So I thought "What does the owner of a real soccer team do?" "He builds a stadium." So I did just that. Well, not exactly a stadium, but a very long table-soccer game. Eleven players on one side, eleven on the other. Eleven white. Eleven black.

There were lots of balls and everyone shouted. It really felt like being at the stadium. Hundreds of goals were scored.

Everyone argued. I was just scared they would break the table. It was a work of art. It was a sculpture. My future began with that stadium. It was the first time the official art world had noticed I was there. My work as an artist started to reap some rewards. I started going to openings. Then came my first artist friends. Then second: my curator friends. Then third friends: the collectors. And then the fourth friends: the gallery owners. None of them ever talked about art, but about "work." What kind of work does he do? What kind of work does she do? What's your work? They asked me and I answered "artist." But they weren't asking about my job, they wanted to know what kind of work I made. Then things got very messy. In fact it was really impossible to explain. I make the "unmakeable," I might have said. Because a soccer team couldn't be a work of art. Actually, I was a framer of sensations, sentiments, moods, positions. If someone told me "I'm a fascist," I thought about how to frame that statement, how to create something you could take home with you. Racism. The soccer team was framed racism, transformed into a big table-soccer game. That was my work.

A work of art I have never been able to frame has always been my way of riding around on a bike. An unfinished work, but still a work. Today people tell me I've sold out. But they don't know what they're saying. To sell out, I'd have to sell myself as I ride around on a bicycle. It is the only thing I do not want to sell and cannot sell, let alone sell out. On a bicycle I never feel illicit. The day I stop riding my bicycle, will also be the day I understand that I have stopped being an artist. In any case, my work, as the others call it, has always been to take my thoughts and those of others and to show them to everyone. There are so many things we think and we don't say, but they still change our way of living, our relationships with others. Like being racist: So many people are racist, but they don't have the guts to say it. Yet even without saying it, they act like racists. So my soccer team was a collective thought. *Raus. Fora da i ball*!

San Pigrus, Patron Saint of Sloth

Sloth is a kind of fear. The characters in the 1958 film, *Big Deal on Madonna Street*, who have always been reference points for me, are not lazy. They work all day to find ways to gain, to pilfer, to survive. They are very active. But in a certain sense they are lazy too—as proven by the famous phrase in the final scene, when Capannelle shouts to Peppe, as the latter is dragged onto a construction site: “Peppe, where the hell are you going? They’ll put you to work!”

Working is different from being active. Working means following rules and schedules, often shoving part of your instinct aside. Sloth is a form of resistance against work as a duty or a necessity. Art is a form of laziness. Though once you are an artist you can never rest again. You can’t say “I’m going to stop being an artist for one week.” Art is a job you have to do 24 hours a day, 7 days a week, 365 days a year. Art puts sloth at the service of the world.

This is why one fine day I decided to invent a grant for an artist to stop being an artist for one full year. I called it the Oblomov Foundation Grant after the titular character of the book by the Russian writer Ivan Goncharov. Oblomov’s laziness is doubt taken to extremes. Since I lived on doubts and extremes, I thought this gentleman deserved to have a foundation named after him. But to make the foundation become a reality I had to raise what was a daunting sum back then of almost twenty million lire. Asking for money is harder work than making it. People who give you money always want something back that is bigger than they gave. If you ask someone for one hundred euros, rest assured they will feel like they've given you ten thousand.

I got on the phone—there were no mobile phones back then—and called everyone I knew that I thought might be able to give me something. At the end of the day, I was exhausted. I had done some pretty boring jobs, but asking for money was the worst of them all. To really punish someone, don't put him or her on a chain gang: make him or her ask people for money all day, eight hours straight. Now that's torture. Explaining the same thing every time: where the hundred euros is supposed to be going. They all asked the same question: "How do I know you're not going to just pocket the dough?" I promised that would not happen. Though later, due to a series of circumstances, I ended up doing just that. Not stealing it, but because I hadn't found a single person willing to stop being an artist for one year. I was the only one who thought he could handle it. The only one with all the qualifications to get the grant. So that's what happened. I banked the money and decided I would move to New York. San Pigrus and Oblomov would watch over me during my journey. But before crossing the ocean, there were other thefts, and other escapes.

Escape Artist

I run away. Since I quit working, I've been escaping. I'm not sure what I am running from, but I am always escaping from someone, from someplace. From myself, a friend told me, who took to psychoanalysis like a duck to water. I started laughing. If there is anyone from whom I'd never try to escape—I even ask him to go with me everywhere, in spite of the risk of getting into ridiculous scrapes—it's me. When I make tracks it's to get out of situations that threaten to eat me up. I have a Mauriziophagy complex. I think everyone wants a piece of me. In some cases I have even checked into a hotel, paid the tab in advance, and then escaped without using the room. I am terrified of obligations. Compulsory schooling was torture for me. Each time I asked my mother if I could go to work like my dad, and she replied that if I didn't go to school the *carabinieri* would put her in jail, I was gripped by anguish. At school I was always tempted to escape. I tried it sometimes, but always got caught by some zealous custodian before I could get out the door.

When I put up the "Be right back" sign I was already trying to transform my flight, my disappearing act, into a work of art. But the thing really clicked when I was invited to do an exhibition in a castle near Turin. The night before the opening all the artists were supposed to sleep over at the castle, but I climbed out the window using a rope of knotted sheets and escaped. That was my work. The knotted sheets hanging out of the window. At first everyone thought I was kidding, but when they realized I was gone, they understood that it was no joke.

Even today many people think what I'm doing is a joke, but my sense of humor is actually pretty weak. When I laugh, it is more a matter of nerves than real amusement. I take my defects and doubts very seriously. I laugh because—as I said—tears are in short supply. If I could cry I'd do it, believe me. The curator, collector, or gallerist who finally manages to make me cry will be the greatest on earth, because maybe he or she will break this spell, this curse of my having become an artist. I'm like Snow White: I've taken a bite of the poisoned apple of art. Until the prince comes along to give me a kiss, and make me digest that piece of apple in my gut, I will never be able to wake up from this hibernation, this lethargy of being an artist. Flight is halfway to slumber, a friend of mine used to say.

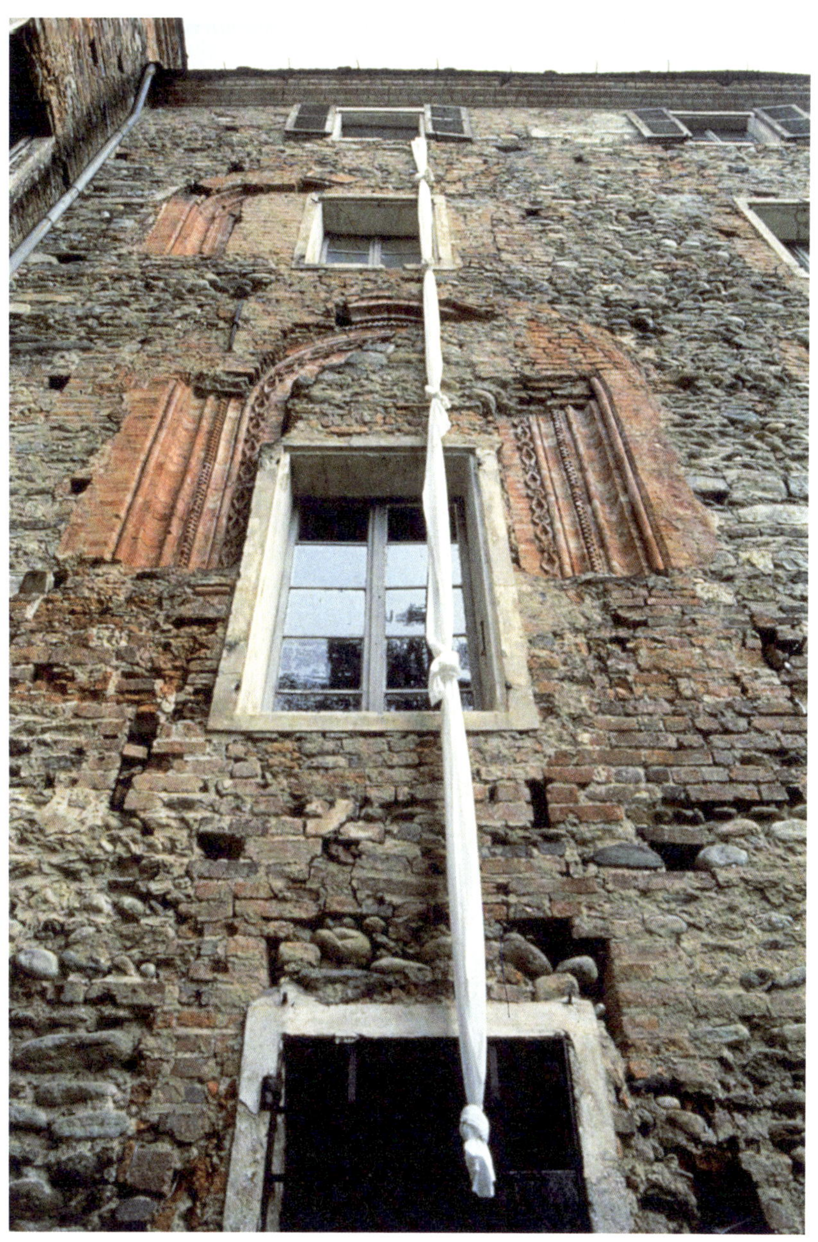

Installation view, *Una domenica a Rivara* (1992)
Castello di Rivara, Centro d'arte contemporanea,
Turin, Italy, 1992

Art Jinx

When I was still in Padua they gave me a nickname: Jinx. It was pinned on me by friends I no longer see for legal reasons—meaning that some of them are in jail and others have left the country to avoid the same fate. I never really understood why they called me that. Maybe I reminded them of some mythical bird: slim at the waist, with long legs, and a large beak. Maybe because when we were traveling together, and would stop to sleep somewhere, they would turn on the light and find me on the bed, awake, eyes open, immobile—like a corpse. I've always enjoyed lying there in the dark with my eyes closed too, without sleeping. After a while I can see everything, even stuff that isn't there. But perhaps the real reason they called me Jinx was because when we were about to do something that stretched the rules a bit I always knew if it would work out well or be a total disaster. I didn't try to jinx things, to bring bad luck. I could just sniff out danger, like a little local Cassandra. Whenever we were plotting something, in the end, somebody always said, "Let's hear what Jinx has to say."

As I mentioned, my heroes were the characters in the *Madonna Street* film by Mario Monicelli. My friends and I resembled them to some extent. We were not a gang, but friends who occasionally organized some activity that ran, let's say, parallel to normal. One of our thrills was to go look at safes either in stores that sold them, or in catalogues. We dreamt of pulling off the heist of the century. Not so much to get rich as to get famous. Really, the strange thing back then was that our obsession wasn't money but breaking out of anonymity, doing something that would wrench us out of our dull existence. We wanted to make headlines. Communication. Since we didn't have a lot of other ideas, and still hadn't thought of making art, the only road was to do something a bit illegal. Nothing really serious, but something that would end up in the pages of *Il Gazzettino*. But for one reason or another, we never made it into the local papers. We made trouble, but not enough of it.

In those days the "autonomists"—experts at getting the front page—took all the wind out of our sails. And our hopes were definitively dashed by the famous wave of *Autonomia Operaia* arrests on April 7, 1979. You couldn't get any press coverage unless you killed somebody. One of my works—a safe that was emptied using a blowtorch—is sort of a monument to what were called the "Years of Lead" and to my friends who never made headlines and never will.

1992: The Discovery of America

I've always been scared of dates. First of all, because you can never remember them, which always gets you into trouble. Anniversaries, birthdays, name days, Valentine's Day, Mother's Day, Father's Day, International Women's Day.

I've always hated streets named after dates. Usually you haven't the faintest idea what the date means, what happened on that hallowed day. They never include the year in the name of the street, like Boulevard April 25, 1887. At least then you could try to guess. But they only put the day and month. The reference could be from the Middle Ages through to the Resistance. It's not fair. So no dates for me, if possible. You may have noticed that in this book, too, I've tried to use dates as little as I can. When you give a date, people start to calculate things and to draw their own conclusions. People who admired you as a great prodigy often change their minds when they find out when you were born, or when you started your art career. It's the same for the works themselves: even they are not spared—the year of birth is essential.

Some artists assign their works a birthday based on when they got the idea. Like seeing a woman and getting the idea of having a kid with her, not managing to do it till five years later, but still saying that the child was born five years before. For artworks, unlike people, being born earlier is an advantage, not a drawback. Growing up early is something to boast about. I don't care about it much. In fact, there are works I did twenty years ago that I would like to be able to make today. Making them now would come in very handy. Unfortunately you can't control ideas, they move around in your head on their own, and come out when you least expect it. Then it is impossible to shove them back where they came from. Once they're out they have to be consumed, like a carton of milk, otherwise they go bad. I've tried using old ideas that had never been finished, and it has always been a waste of time. Like going back to old girlfriends in the hope that things will be different. If things are different, they've only gotten worse.

So I'd rather let dates run their course, live their own life. But even if we forget that years exist, now and then we have to remember at least one. The year I cannot possibly forget is 1992. That year I took a deep breath, pocketed the Oblomov Grant, and crossed the Atlantic to reach New York. 1992. Without that year I wouldn't be here, or there, for that matter. I wouldn't be any place. My English sucked and I knew almost nobody. The advantage, though, was that no one knew me either. I could move around freely and do whatever popped into my head. For the first time in my life, I felt like I was in a place from which there was no need to escape. Because nobody really gives a damn if you are there or not.

I went to live in the East Village—a rented room where I remained for at least ten years, and could have stayed another ten. But when a bit of success rolls in you kid yourself that you can change your way of being, and you start doing things you would never normally have done, and never should have tried to do, like moving house, for instance. But that's another story.

1992. The wardrobe was the first thing to tackle. New York was heaven for somebody used to a recycled existence. In what was considered the trash you could find almost-new things, like my sky blue running jacket, which was to become my first uniform. I found it outside the home of a gentleman who would become one of my best friends—an Italian curator who had lived in New York for many years. We were introduced in an Argentinian cafe called Novecento by a mutual friend, a painter from the Tyrol in northern Italy. One of my first "famous" works is titled *Novecento* (1997)—the dangling horse with stretched legs. I don't remember if I chose the title in honor of that café that changed my life a little, or if it was a tribute to the film by Bernardo Bertolucci. Yes, my life changed quite a bit in that café, because thanks to the curator and the painter, I managed to worm my way into the New York art world, which looked like an impregnable fortress from the outside.

To be honest, even today the art world of that city seems impenetrable to me: an island with its own laws, its own moral rules that seem unbelievably strange, absurd, and at times incomprehensible to Europeans and, in particular, Italians. Even now, inside the fortress I have the sensation of being viewed askance, considered a "jester"—the guy the king needs for a good laugh now and then—but only now and then. For the rest of the time, he is ignored and snubbed. Today, I still have the sensation of being very tiny compared to this big castle to which I have gained entry. Like my *Mini-me* (1999), I feel as if I'm perched on the shelf of life watching the people who pass by below me. I feel like Pinocchio's Talking Cricket, always in danger, not because I say anything special but because my presence is annoying. If some critic had a big enough hammer he would crush me. He would squash me on the wall of art history, making me into a little stain that would gradually fade with time.

The critics think I showed up here with my art to judge them, to challenge them, to suggest that they stop telling lies about art and artists. They don't really know what I'm talking about, so they prefer not to listen. Maurizio! All they have to do is say my name and a big smile comes to their lips, or they even chuckle, and they feel satisfied. They cannot ignore me, the way the *Gazzettino* did in Padua during the "Years of Lead." They have to take note of my existence, and my art. In spite of themselves, they cannot avoid listening to my artistic jokes. But they cannot get beyond the New York art world where artists never laughed, but got drunk in some dive, and sometimes even killed themselves to boot. Compared to that art world, I'm like a cartoon. A fake character that ought to go away when you turn off the TV. But the art world is a TV that is always on. Even the most serious critics and curators are sometimes forced to look at the children's shows, with the puppets and the cartoons.

In 1992, I did not think about all this. I looked at the castle and rode around it on my bicycle. Every so often, thanks to my friends from the Novecento café, I managed to get into the courtyard and see one of the princes pass, with his entourage of nobles. Back then, it was easy to laugh someone like me off the stage. The hero at the time was this young fellow who would get naked, cover himself with Vaseline, and try to climb the walls of the gallery, filmed all the while by video cameras: a sort of human fly, a Spiderman. A far cry from escaping from a window with knotted bedclothes, like in a Buster Keaton film, *n'est pas*? Here you needed muscles to climb the walls, to reach the upper levels of the castle, where the critics and curators bowed down to the heroes and emperors of a world I had never seen before, not even on postcards.

It was 1992. The usual slice of bread with margarine got dipped into my cup of *caffè latte*. But everything had a different taste. I had arrived. Even though, without being told, I knew I still had to set forth. It never gets completely dark in New York. In the room where I lived, there was always at least some light. I lay there with my eyes open, but Jinx was gone. I had become some other creature.

Back to My Troubles

America was good for me. But after a while, I got a strange feeling of homesickness. It was strange because I didn't have a home. All I remember about the trip back was an urgent need to go to the bathroom a few minutes before landing. The plane was full and I was sandwiched between two people. I wanted to get up but the flight attendant yelled at me to stay put. That wasn't an option, though, because I was really going to wet my pants. So I hid what I was doing under the little airline-issue blanket and took a leak in an almost empty bottle of mineral water. Then I hid it in my backpack.

At customs they told me to empty out the contents of the pack. When I put the bottle on the table, the customs guy looked at me and asked what it was. I told him the truth, but he thought I was pulling his leg and barked, "Drink it!" I looked at him, and then it was my turn to ask him if he was kidding. He told me he was completely serious and if I didn't drink it he would take me into an office and make me stay there until the contents of the bottle had been analyzed. People think up all kinds of crazy ways to smuggle drugs. I understood there was no way out, so I obeyed, taking a gulp of my piss. "Welcome back!" I thought.

In New York I had forgotten about all my troubles, but when I got back I realized what a state I was in, especially from a financial point of view. And I also realized something about the state of Italy. The customs incident reminded me of two artworks I had made when I had no idea what to do. Today, looking back, people consider them subversive, and they complain that I am no longer as courageous as I was at the start of my life as an artist. But I've never been courageous at all. I even wear seatbelts in taxis. When I got a medical certificate as an excuse not to participate in a group show and then showed it as an artwork, I did it because the very idea of making an artwork made me feel sick. For an artist, a shortage of ideas, combined with shortage of cash, is at least the equivalent of a case of bronchitis. Another time, when I didn't know what to put in a show, I went to the police station and reported the theft of an invisible artwork. The cop filed the report without even blinking. I wondered—I still wonder—if that policeman didn't know the meaning of the word invisible, or if the idea of art was so foreign to him that the existence of an invisible artwork didn't seem the least bit strange. This was the world to which I had returned.

Milan was up in arms about the "Mani Pulite" investigations, a huge political corruption scandal. But I didn't care much about what was going on, it was off radar for me. America and New York had changed me. I wanted to go back there as quickly as possible. America has an incredible grip on people's imagination. When you return from there, everyone looks at you differently, maybe with a little bit of respect. If you are an artist and you go to America, everyone thinks you are half hero and half nuts. In any case, as soon as I got back from the States I met a rather chubby gentleman who said he had an art gallery. I'd heard about him. He took me to a restaurant near Porta Venezia, and over lunch he proposed that I do a show at his place. I looked at him and said alright, but first we have to make a bet. "What kind of a bet?" I bet him that he would not be able to sell my work. "What work?" A ballpoint pen with no ink left in it. It was no simple task. I pulled out the pen and handed it over.

He took it, but after a week he called me and said nobody wanted it. The price was too high. I think it was 1.5 million lire. "That's a shame," I said. But a couple of days later I showed up at the gallery with a collector, and I managed to sell him the inkless pen. The gallerist had lost the bet, but we decided to do the show together anyway, but only on the condition that during the two days prior to the opening no one could go to the gallery—not even him.

On the morning of the day the show was to open, when the gallerist came to the gallery he was faced with an unpleasant surprise. The door had been walled up. There was just a little opening so you could peer inside. He was unnerved and thought the idea was idiotic. But then, he looked through the peephole and saw that every so often, on a rope stretched across the space inside, a mechanical bear would ride by, balanced on a tricycle. One of the best memories of my career is the way he laughed—the sight of his joy in that moment. I realized I had found the right idea. You can't know that the idea is right by whether the work sells or not. You have to look at the eyes of people when they see the work. Seeing wonder in the eyes of someone who is looking at what you were afraid was crap might just be the biggest gift an artist can receive from a work. But the opposite is also true. The more famous you get, the more success you have, the more the smiles on people's faces become plastic and automatic. Then, even if you really do make crap, everyone has the same reaction of fake wonder that is as painful as the real wonder was pleasurable.

Back then, though, I wasn't famous at all, so I couldn't judge the different nuances in the smile and eyes of a viewer. I was innocent. The fear of failure was real, because it was not a fear that had to do with the reaction of a limited group of people. If the gallerist hadn't laughed, my defeat would have been total, definitive. There would have been no possibility of redemption of the kind I would be granted, as the years passed, even when I made blatant mistakes. On that Thursday morning, what was at stake was my art learner's permit. I was that little bear on the high wire. I was the one who ran the risk of crashing to the ground. It was my first self-portrait.

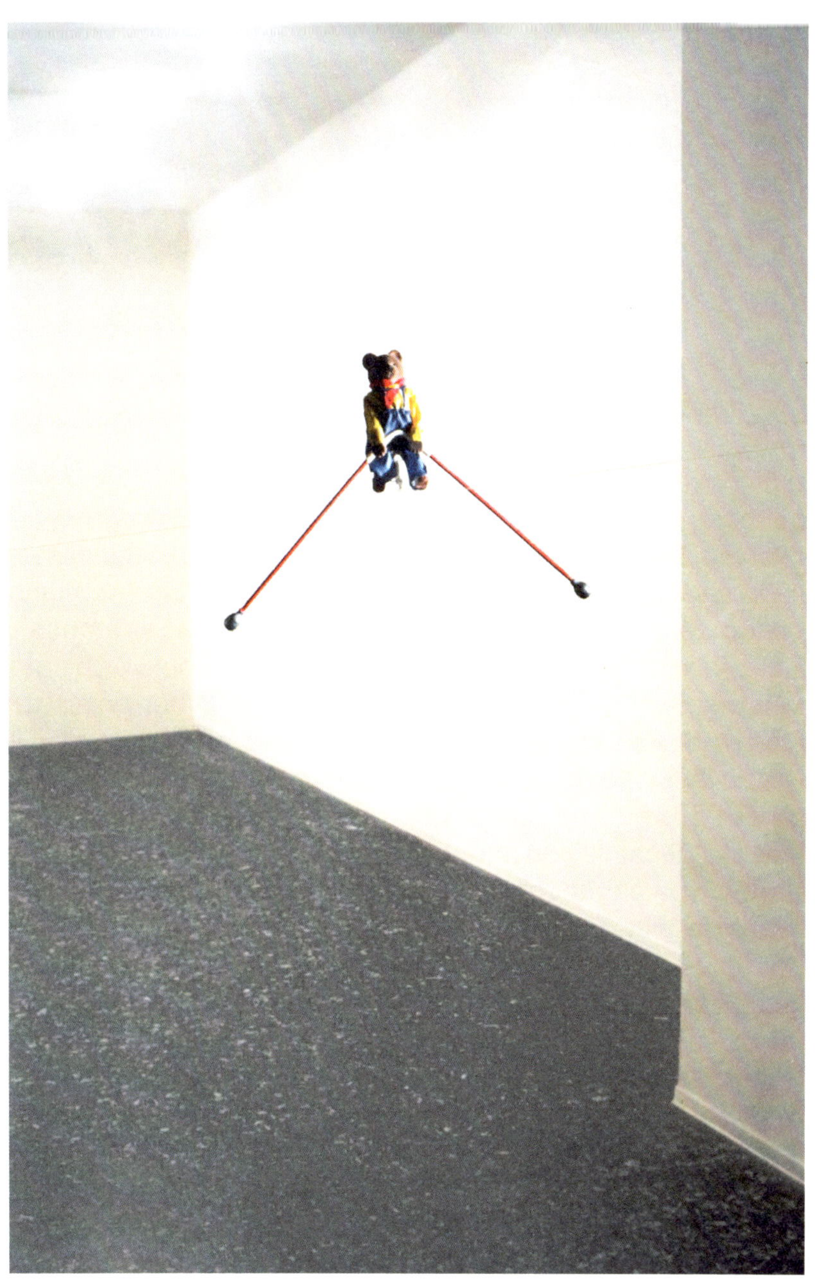

Installation view, *Untitled* (1993)
Massimo De Carlo, Milan, 1993

In the Arena with the Lions

An artist's career is like a tightrope walker's rope, only the rope is very long. So long, that you can tell where it starts, but not where it ends. Artists walk the rope and know that once the journey has begun there is no turning back. They know they might make it, or that they might fall. Better not look down. For two reasons. First, because the chasm might be too deep. Second, because the rope might be stretched just a few inches above the ground, and that would be a sign that the destiny in store was nothing special. When an artist stays too close to the ground, it is very hard to kiss the sky. I've never looked down. I've never looked forward. I have always walked with my eyes closed. You should never look forward because you might discover that someone else is in front of you on the rope, and it is impossible to pass unless they lose their balance and fall off. Every artist, to have any hope of success, has to believe in the illusion that he or she is the only one on the rope. When the illusion fades, because we make the mistake of opening our eyes, all that is left is to hope that those in front of us will go crashing to the ground.

Have I ever wished an artist would fall? I don't recall having done so, as the former prime minister, Giulio Andreotti, would say. But maybe I could say "I guess not," though I don't know if such an answer would be accepted in a court of law. The little bear on the tricycle brought me luck, because for the duration of the exhibition he never fell off the wire. A record. The idea of closing up the door to the gallery with a wall of bricks came to me as I was thinking about the worst sensation you can have in life: that of being shut out, of being excluded from a place you want to go. Excluded from discos, restaurants, offices. A reverse prison. I imagined the horrible sensation of finding the door to your house walled up. It would be even worse if there was a hole, and you could see that someone else was living or doing something in there. At the same time, there was a desire to keep people away from my ideas, my thoughts, me.

Today people think this fear of being recognized has something to do with the fact that I have become somewhat famous. I admit there is some truth in that. But actually this fear had begun to grow in me when I was still in Padua, when together with my crew, we did unsavory things, and didn't want to be recognized afterwards. I still remember the fear that gripped me when I saw someone staring at me in a store or on the street. I immediately thought I'd been recognized, that they had seen me someplace where I had pilfered or misappropriated something, or expropriated it, as they said in those days—not so much for the proletariat as out of my own damned indigence. The reasons behind my forays into the ideology of self-help had more to do with plain poverty than with class struggle.

My struggle had been *in* class, in elementary and middle school, and I had often paid the price. I had no intention of doing any more struggling in any class for the rest of my days. In those days you didn't steal things, you took possession of basic needs. One very effective method was to pick out a big pot at the supermarket, fill it up with victuals, and then go to the checkout and pay only for the pot. This trick worked every time. But I was left with the anxiety that sooner or later someone would recognize me and make me pay for what I had taken. So this paranoia grew, and I've been trying to hide ever since. At times by using other people in my place, even at times by wearing a disguise, though I have always hated carnival time and costume parties—I think they are humiliating.

I accumulated all these fears and discomforts inside me, and at a certain point I decided to share them with others. Well, maybe "share" isn't the right word. I decided that other people should have to go through what I had to go through in life. There was a period, I don't know why, in which I had gotten it into my head that I was a victim of society, its rules, conventions, and laws. An obsession that later switched into a desire to transform everyone with whom I came into contact into a victim: from women to art dealers, curators to other artists. I felt like I was in the arena, together with the lions that wanted to eat me.

There were two gallerists who wanted at all costs to do a show with me after they had seen the balancing bear. I had no ideas, but they insisted, and in the end I said OK. They were pleased until they found out that the exhibition would consist of them dressed up in lion costumes for its duration. One day when I was watching Walt Disney's *Jungle Book* (1967), a lightbulb went off in my head. If you transform people into animals and animals into people, there is the possibility that one time out of two you will manage to do something good. The two gallerist lions were perfect.

Two years later I was to repeat the same operation, but this time I dressed the gallerist up as a big pink dick with bunny ears. I got the idea because instead of talking about art, the guy always talked about sex. At the time I wasn't getting much of the latter, since I was born erotically shy. This young fellow who boasted of his XXX-ploits embarrassed me, like those friends who told me of their erotic adventures when I was still a virgin, taking for granted that I must know what they were talking about. I had my revenge. The pink dick costume. I had forced the gallerist to wear his obsession. I had turned him inside out like a sock. Those who entered the gallery could see his mania, in the form of art. The gallery was a set-up, a trap to catch girls. But now the girls who showed up were laughing their heads off instead of being charmed by the young dealer. I had taken

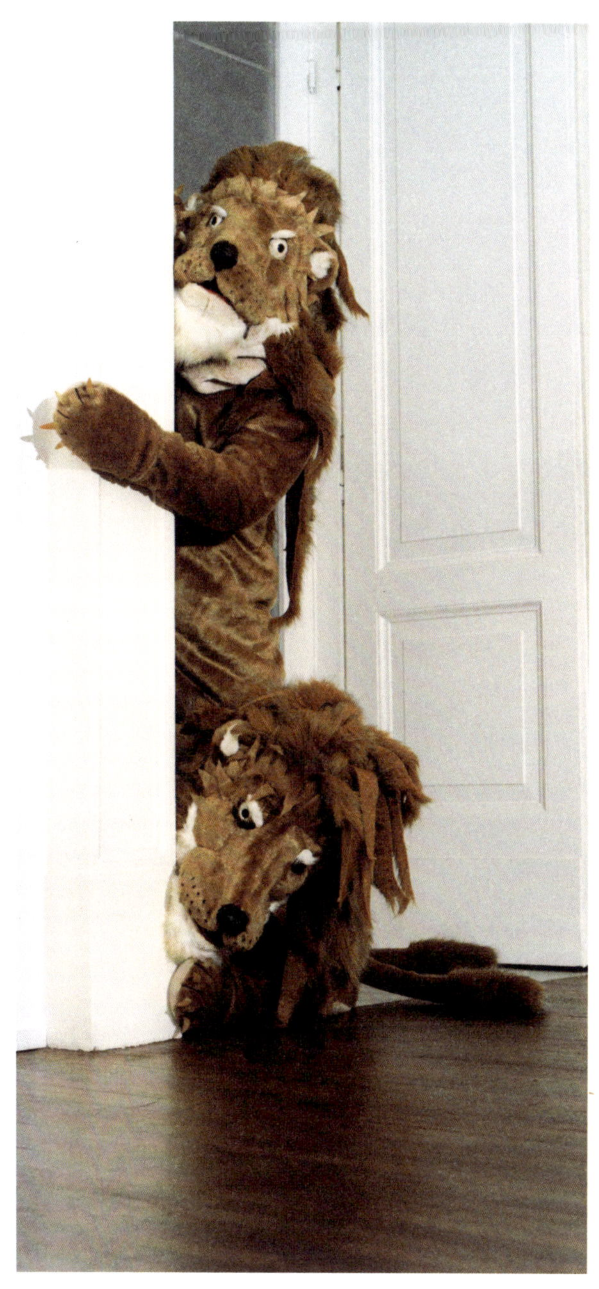

Tarzan & Jane (1993)
Galleria Raucci/Santamaria, Naples, Italy, 1993

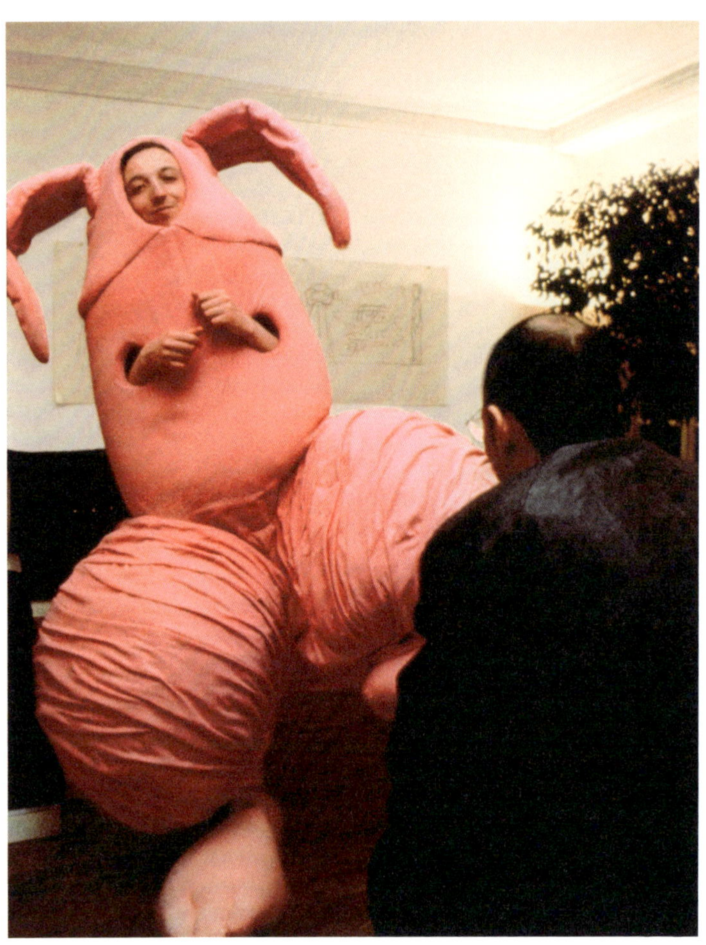

***Errotin le vrai lapin* (1995)**
Perrotin, Paris, 1995

my revenge, humiliating him—without knowing that after a few years, after having gained a bit of success and a little money, I too would use art and my artist status as bait for women I wanted. Today, I'm the one who should wear the pink costume. Once again, unwittingly, I had created a self-portrait, a posteriori.

You Never Forget the First Scent

During my first year in New York, every week I climbed four flights of stairs to visit my friend the curator, who lived close by. He made the same minestrone for lunch and we ate it, together with his daughter who was two or three years old. Every week, a regular routine. We talked a lot about everything and seldom about art. But one day when I arrived, he was all excited. They had asked him to curate a small part of the "Open" section for young artists at the Biennale di Venezia. In those days there were no mobile phones, no email, and all the rest. If you were lucky, you had a fax machine. He had one. He showed me a piece of paper with faded ink where they were asking him to curate that section. I have never asked anyone to invite me to an exhibition, but it was clear that I wanted to be invited to the biennale. It was also clear that he wanted to invite me. It was a unique chance for both of us. I was invited. My first biennale.

I went on to do the Biennale di Venezia six more times. For some reason, I have never been at my best in a biennale. I've never understood why. I feel the pressure of the big event too much, where everyone is looking for the mistakes in the exhibition and by the artist. The biennale is always a missed opportunity. You could say something, but you end up saying little or nothing. The first time is the hardest, though. Even more so in my case, because I was already considered a joker who escapes, who makes curators and spectators uncomfortable. I already had a lousy reputation by the time I did my first biennale.

When I reached the Rope Walk of the Arsenale, the spaces were completely empty. My friend showed me where my work would be placed. I looked around and asked him if a space up between the columns, was free. "Of course it's free, who would want to put a work up there?" "I would." I'll do it. Actually, as usual, I had no idea what to put there. As always, I needed money to make ends meet. The biennale was a big chance for an artist, but first of all I needed chances to be a human. A few weeks before the opening, the curator kept calling me to find out what I had decided to show. Whenever I could, I avoided answering the phone, and when he finally caught me I invented the weirdest, most absurd excuses. My friend got angry and threatened to pull the piece, though he knew I wouldn't believe him. He didn't even believe himself. At a certain point, though, there was no more time: I had to decide, but I really had no ideas. In such instances, I used to go back to see my friend from the store in Milan where I slept when I was homeless. He always welcomed me with open arms and often gave me ideas that later became works. This time, however, even he was fresh out of clever inventions. People who want to criticize what I do often say my works are just simple, even banal, smart-ass ideas. But that evening, after consuming many beers and many cigarettes, we couldn't even hatch one smart gimmick. I was desperate. Time to escape again? Nothing doing, this was the biennale, I would be kicked out of the art world forever. The biennale is like Alcatraz. There is no escape.

The clock struck 2am and our brains, like the bottles and glasses on the table, were completely empty. We went out into the fresh air of a spring night in Milan, and as we were walking, who knows where to, my friend told me: "You might as well just sell your spot in the biennale." He laughed. But I wasn't laughing. The next morning I was already at an advertising agency, to offer my space at the biennale as a promotional opportunity to any company that might be interested. A couple of days went by and nobody took the bait, until finally a gentleman called me who represented a perfume company. He said they would be interested in using my space to launch a new fragrance and asked me how much it would cost. We agreed on a price. I signed a sort of contract and it looked like a done deal. Two days before the opening, the company installed a huge poster. Everyone thought it was my work, and I was careful not to clue them in. I think that selling a piece of the biennale without permission, at least in those days, was illegal.

When the biennale opened everyone ignored the poster. Everyone ignored my presence. I had blown a big chance. But I had a few million lire in my pocket, which was some consolation. I bought a very small flat in a big tenement inhabited mostly by drug dealers and hookers. I thought I could kiss my art ambitions goodbye, that I would never set foot in the biennale again. But I was wrong. In any case, I plunged into deep summer hibernation. The smell of that American minestrone that could have changed my life, and which I missed very much, wafted up my nostrils. But I had achieved something: I had become—and I think I still am—the only artist to ever get paid for having a space at the Biennale di Venezia.

The Bimbo and the Bomb

It was a monastic summer after the biennale. But once again, luck was with me, so I made a little sacrificial vow: no sex till September. Lady Luck responded on July 27, 1993. At night I always rode around Milan on my bicycle, and that night was no exception. But that time I wasn't alone. I was with a girl who also had a bicycle. One of the best places to ride was in the public gardens on Via Palestro. You had to find a hole in the fence. At night the park was empty, you could listen to the crunch of the gravel under your wheels. I did it often by myself, but that time I was with a girl, and I didn't want to ruin a chance for romance with some risky business that might not pan out. I decided to change the route, to ride by the cathedral. When we were at the door to my building, as I was awkwardly trying to kiss the girl, I heard a big bang. We paid no attention, as by now we were really kissing. Maybe we went up to my place, I don't remember, or I'd rather not remember.

The next day, on the radio, they said that the bang was a car bomb that had exploded near PAC, the Padiglione d'Arte Contemporanea, which was right there where I always took my solitary bike rides. So maybe a woman saved my life. For the first time, and maybe the last one too. My relationships with women have always complicated my life and perhaps disturbed theirs. But never has the desire for a kiss brought the kind of luck it brought that night.

I went to the site of the bombing. All that was left was rubble. Five people had lost their lives, but for some reason

I thought there had only been three victims. That whole fall I kept thinking about what our destiny is made of—the taste of our luck or our misfortune. I thought about it day and night. My luck had the taste of violet lipstick. The misfortune of the poor victims had the taste of plaster and rubble.

When I was asked to do a show in a gallery in London, I remembered all those fall meditations and decided to make a little monument to the victims of Via Palestro, one of whom was a guy from Morocco who was sleeping on a park bench. There were five victims, but I kept forgetting two of them. The number three was stuck in my head. Maybe because it was useful for me to have only one more T in the neon sign with my name. In fact, the three Ts of "Catttelan" became three crosses, and then in a burlap bag I stuck a sizeable quantity of the rubble from PAC, which I had gotten hold of in a rather adventurous way. That was my monument. I immediately became a political artist. The most *engagé* part of the art world flocked to my support. Some put forward the notion that I might be the true heir of Arte Povera, the most politicized art movement of the postwar era. Others called my little monument a sort of contemporary version of Picasso's *Guernica* (1937).

I kept my mouth shut as tightly as possible, and when asked to comment I sent a friend to do it by phone, saying anything that came into his head. I felt very Peter Sellers in *Being There* (1979). I didn't really know what I was doing, let alone what little I was saying. Yet every time I lifted a finger an avalanche of interpretations, so to speak, came down. Lots of noise, not much money. The situation didn't seem to really change. I sold the rubble monument and went back to New York.

The Donkey That Made the Golden Sausage

Home sweet home. I really did feel right at home in my rented room. In New York my needs seemed to shrink to an even more minimal minimum than in Milan. I could live on two dollars a day. The biennale had left no trace. No one had noticed I was there. The few who noticed said the work was banal, or already seen elsewhere. Maybe my little idea really was banal, but not seen elsewhere. In New York I was a nobody again. My curator friend and painter friend were back, too. They introduced me to a young dealer who had just opened a space below SoHo next to a German gallerist—an unbearable idiot. The young dealer suggested doing a show, and I agreed. As usual, I had no ideas. Every morning I ate a bagel, hoping to get a nice, round, chewy idea. I went swimming, hoping that after my laps I might emerge dripping with ideas. I even tried going back to eat more minestrone at the curator's house. But the ideas did not come, the show was fast approaching, and the dealer wanted to know what I had in mind.

I proposed knocking down the wall of the nasty German dealer's gallery and doing a show that was identical to the one he was doing, like a mirror image. This idea was rejected, first by the German, and then by my gallerist. We were back to zilch. But then I remembered that exhibition in the 1960s, where Jannis Kounellis, one of the Arte Povera group, put horses in a gallery as if it were a stable. I've never been much of a thoroughbred. If anything I was a bit of a donkey—at

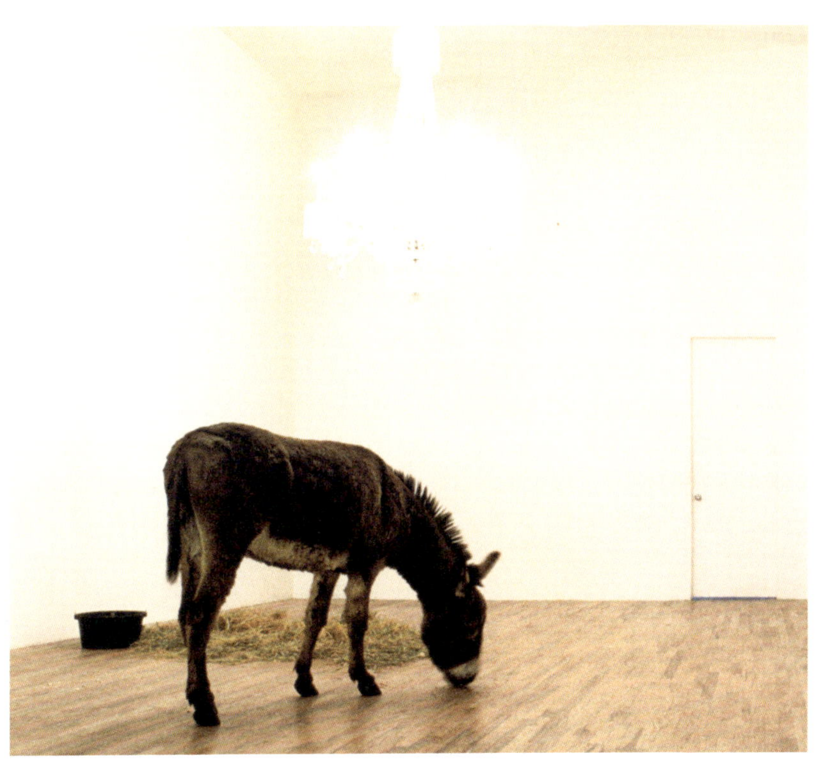

Installation view, *Warning! Enter at your own risk. Do not touch, do not feed, no smoking, no photographs, no dogs, thank you* (1994)
Daniel Newburg Gallery, New York, 1994

least at school. I thought that might do the trick, so my exhibition was a donkey eating hay in the gallery. To make it a little more interesting, in the "stall" I hung a crystal chandelier, which added a touch of nobility to the poor beast, which was even more out of place than me in the art world.

The turnout for the opening was disappointing. Nobody seemed very interested or very upset. Some guy asked me if I knew about the show Kounellis had done. My exhibition was a flop. Even floppier, because during the night the donkey started to bray, the neighbors called the cops, and the gallerist was ordered to remove the animal in the wee hours of the morning.

The work was gone, but the show was supposed to run for a month. All I could do was to find a replacement for the donkey. A string of sausages. Those who entered the gallery asked what it was all about. First there was a donkey. Then it was gone. People saw the sausages and thought the donkey was dead. The donkey was just fine, alive and well and out in the country, near New York. The show was a disaster in the sense that nobody paid any attention to it at all. Yet I had made a step forward. No one had seen me come in, but I had managed to sneak my way into the New York art world, and I wasn't about to let them kick me back out, try as they might.

Who the Hell Are You?

Nobody had ever heard of me outside Italy. Maybe someone had in Paris, thanks to a rather plump girlfriend of mine. She was a fox and a great cook, and treated me to a diet of food and sex that left me listless for weeks on end. For me, New York was like a health spa: regenerating. I was part of that shapeless blob of artists in search of visibility, success, and maybe even money. I got by on two bucks a day, but I was starting to feel the pinch. My method was simple. I went all over the place until the moment for spending money arose. Then I went home. At home I thought about how many people you meet in your life, how many of them you remember, and how you remember them.

Once, years before leaving Italy, I had conducted this experiment on myself. How many of the people I had met could remember who I was and what I looked like? I invited as many as possible to go, one at a time, to see a guy who worked for the police making Identi-Kit images of criminals. My acquaintances went there and tried to provide a description of me. Based on their recollections, the guy did a pencil drawing. In the end I had all these portraits. Some of them looked like me, while in others I was unrecognizable. I made it into a work called *Super-Noi* (1995–99). Because there's you, but there are also all these people who have a different idea about that "you," so in the end the "you" becomes an "us" (*noi*). I think our character is composed of this "us" made of lots of "yous." Even if we are always ourselves, every time we meet someone we slightly or drastically adjust to that other person, in the things we say, the way we move. All these adjustments can't help but have an effect on our personality. We are us, but we are also a little bit the others. Just as the others are also a little bit us.

New York was a sort of peephole into my personality. Since almost nobody knew me, I had to adjust less, and I had a chance to find myself again—the self that I had left behind that morning in Padua and rarely got a chance to meet. In New York it happened, not so often, but it happened, even though speaking English was a dreadful effort, since my way of expressing myself was very often impossible to translate. When I couldn't manage to translate what I wanted to say I relied on my body, like a marionette. To make myself understood I moved my body with the strings of my thoughts, trying to use the smallest possible number of words. This is why even today many people see me as a sort of clown, an acrobat, and my art as a bag of jester's tricks played for laughs at the king's court. Actually, I started out very different: much stiffer, much more closed. I had no choice but to soften up, to avoid acting completely paralyzed and mute.

Global Ant

I'm an ant. I like to hoard. I like to gather ideas so I can use them when they are in short supply. After my first exhibition in New York the ideas seemed to be already finished. My show in Paris was recycled from the one I did with the lion costumes in Naples two years earlier. I forced the gallerist, as I already said, to dress up as a big penis. Then came the first invitation to a biennial far away from Italy, in Korea, and after a sixteen-hour trip they told me my work was too expensive to ship from Italy. I tried getting mad but got nowhere. I was a pawn on the art chessboard. So I asked to see the room I was supposed to show in. It was a big space. I said OK, I'd think of something. I would make it there, in the three days left before the opening.

I concentrated and brought forth the ant that lives inside me. I went back to the room. I asked them to turn off all the lights, leaving only a small spotlight at the center of the room. Then I took a little plastic ant out of my pocket, which I had bought at a local market. I put it at the center of the room in the small circle of light. But it wasn't just any ant. My ant was pissed off. With his little legs, he gestured to anyone curious enough to cross the darkness of the empty room and approach the center, to fuck off.

It was my message to the curators of the exhibition, the organizers, but also the viewers. I had traveled from one side of the planet to the other, only to find my work wasn't there. I got my revenge by telling people to go to hell who had come from who knows where to see my work. I had become a global ant. I would travel far and wide, but I would never get shafted like that again.

Melanconicus

I was becoming melancholy. I had the feeling I was getting nowhere, spinning my gears. Some cash was finally coming in, but it was uphill all the way. My apartment in Milan was like a shoebox. Feeling desperate one day, I used a chisel to remove a few inches of wall, to add a few square feet. Instead of 170 I now had 190 square feet. It was satisfying. A conquest, like those countries that are proud to have picked up a few yards of territory in some war or other. My war was with myself. I never seemed to gain any ground. Every work was a battle, but I never seemed to win the war. Ever. Like a prisoner I had scraped my walls in an attempt to escape, once again, from a suffocating situation. I did my second show in Milan. I did a second one in London. In Milan I hung a stuffed horse from the ceiling. I got the idea looking at photos of horses being loaded onto ships during World War I. Actually, though, it was yet another self-portrait. I felt powerless, hanging off the world with no chance of making even the slightest difference. Just meat for the curators and critics.

Then I reached London, and the sense of malaise got even worse. There were people like Damien Hirst who were already making millions with their art. I felt like a cyclist in the Giro d'Italia, at the bottom of the climb up the Passo del San Gottardo, looking at the front of the pack, almost at the top already. Or like a Formula 1 driver who never really manages to figure out where he is on the track. He might think he's winning, only to find out he's already been lapped, or vice versa. I thought I'd been lapped more than once. In London my despair came to a head. I had a kind of dream. I was back in the dining room of my home in Padua. It was cold. The sink was full of dirty dishes. Outside there was fog, and I was sitting at the table, alone. Everyone was dead. Parents, sisters, friends. Now it's your turn, I thought, as I woke up.

The dream was my new work. Like *Cinderella* but with a bad ending. The title, in fact, was a bit like that word the Fairy Godmother says in the Walt Disney version. Only I couldn't remember the word, so the story had an unhappy ending. My work is actually the tragic ending of a story. The story of a poor squirrel left all alone, maybe burdened with debt, who finds a pistol and kills himself in his shabby kitchen, leaving everything around him dirty. I thought this work would be the last nail in my artist's coffin. Instead, like that time with the toy bear when I saw the gallerist laughing, this time I went to the gallery and found a girl sitting next to the work, crying. She was crying with joy, not sadness. She thought the work was tender and very beautiful, at the same time. This work has become one of my most famous pieces, one of the ones most often requested for exhibitions and books. I had pushed a precise button in the viewer's soul, the way Disney did with his cartoon. Yet it was a pessimistic work that banished all hope even from the carefree spirit of animals.

I looked at the group of artist winners reaching the summit, and behind me I saw an even faster competitor who didn't want to let me escape. It was poverty. I struggled my way up, but so did poverty. Still too hot on my trail. Without my nightmares and paranoia I would never have made any works. To end up homeless—now that's scary. So, for an exhibition in Turin I came up with two figures that seemed like real hoboes.

In New York I was constantly struck by the way certain bums always stay in the same place, becoming urban landmarks. When your local bum vanishes, you always think the worst. My two bums, *Andreas e Mattia* (1996), were sleeping,

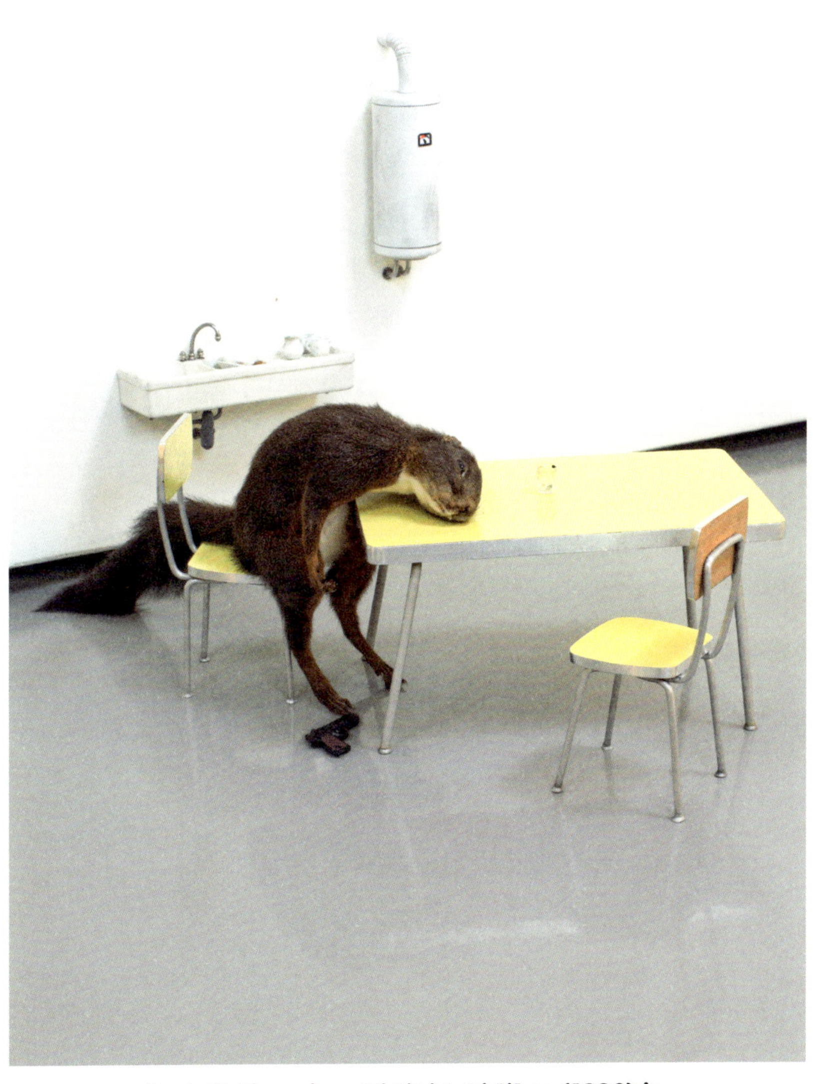

Installation view, *Bidibidobidiboo* (1996) in *Italics. Arte italiana fra tradizione e rivoluzione 1968–2008*, Palazzo Grassi, Venice, 2008

and I put them in the courtyard of the Galleria d'Arte Moderna in Turin when no one could see me do it. On the morning before the opening, I saw an ambulance and a police car in front of the gate. I asked what was happening and they told me there was a homeless man who must be dead. In the morning the superintendent had seen the guy, and had kindly brought him a cappuccino and a brioche, but the man didn't move. The poor super called for help, thinking the man must have bitten the dust. I didn't have the heart to tell them the truth. In the end I confessed that it was an artwork, and I had to put up with some angry insults. But I had scored again. I saw the world through the eyes of defeat. Yet from that vantage point, it seemed like I was managing to win more and more victories. The theory of the power of positive thinking didn't seem to work for me. The more I saw and pulled out the dark sides of my life and those of society, the more I seemed to meet with success. I was becoming the servant of my own melancholy, it had become my agent, and a very skillful negotiator of my relationships with the outside world.

Back to Madonna Street

Sometimes, thinking about my life in Padua, I would feel kind of homesick. Back then the battle was with one day at a time, not with ideas, art, and those who had more success than you. We dared the day to try boring us. We almost always won. And that was enough for us to go to bed feeling satisfied. Now satisfaction had to be earned the hard way. It never came at the end of the day, and if it did arrive it would be after a week, maybe a month of waiting. Most of the time disappointment came knocking.

When they invited me to show in a museum in Amsterdam, I was caught in a moment of memories and thoughts of the past. As usual, I didn't have the slightest idea what to show in this exhibition with other artists. But I was counting on the night, on the tips from the dark side that seemed to always come to me. The day before, I had visited a dreadful exhibition in a gallery in the city. When I saw it my first impulse was to destroy everything. But why destroy when everything can be transformed and improved to become something that is yours? So, the next morning, I got the idea of stealing the whole exhibition and presenting it at the museum as my own work. The real job would be to organize the heist. I rediscovered the excitement and enthusiasm of bygone days. With a van and some accomplices, we broke into the gallery at night, through a window, and stole everything. Everything. There was nothing left, not even the electrical sockets. It was all going smoothly, but then someone saw us and called the cops. We got nabbed. But art is the perfect alibi. I highly recommend it to anyone who wants to pull off a crime. Later, you just say it was an artwork, and you'll probably get off scot free, which is what happened to us. I had taken Picasso literally when he said that good artists copy but geniuses steal. I was a genius. Though after that I have stayed within the limits of the good artist, copying as much as possible, hoping the professors don't catch me. It almost always works. Almost.

Fakers and Fakes

I had run the risk of Dutch prison. But crime paid, in terms of fame. The art world had seen me from a new angle. I had become a sort of Robin Hood who steals from the rich galleries to help the poor museums. What's more, I had paid tribute to teamwork, debunking the myth of the egomaniac artist who wants to do it all alone. Except for living, I have always tried to do nothing at all by myself. I even dedicated one of my sculptures, the one that said that love saves your life, to friendship and cooperation: an idea lifted straight out of the Brothers Grimm and transformed into an artwork. The donkey, dog, cat, and rooster, one atop the other, all emitting their own sound. In the original fable, these animals work together to beat an enemy and win back their freedom.

For me, art has always worked a bit like that. You can achieve freedom and defeat the enemy together, in a group, kidding around, laughing, fighting. Not like a political group or an art movement, but exactly like a band of friends or thieves. A togetherness that is not based on personal interests, but on a shared harmony. Every so often the band messes up the rhythm, one of the players goes away or gets kicked out. It happens. What counts is to keep on playing, with the same spirit.

I could talk about it like a soccer coach or a great striker. If I have gotten to where I am today, it is because I owe it all to teamwork. The titles of my works always come from conversations, phone calls, emails. But even the works happen by talking to people, to close and perfidious friends. So after the failed heist, people started to invite me to show here and there. I'd made it, you might think. Think again. They invited me because they could smell something burning. But nobody really wanted to get burned. I was no longer an outsider or an insider: I was just a sider, someone who stays off to one side.

When they invited me to Vienna, to the famous Secession, they tossed me into the basement. I was there but not there. The cowards, I thought. I'll show them. I took two bicycles, stuck them on two trestles planted in the floor, and attached the pedals to the building's electrical supply. Then I took the guards and told them they would have to pedal, in shifts. No pedaling, no light. They agreed, so when people visited the show they would notice that the light came and went, varying in its intensity. It depended on how tired or lazy the guards were. Art is entirely a question of energy invested and energy wasted. My art career is a bit like the lightbulbs in Vienna. The light comes and goes. It depends on how hard I pedal, but also on how much the people around me are willing to pedal. There are certain months when an outrageous art bill comes in, because too many ideas have been consumed. Other months the bill is low, not much has been produced or consumed. There are even months when I should get a refund, because I haven't consumed even one idea, though actually lots of them have gone elsewhere.

In 1997, the bills were way too big. After Vienna I was invited to Venice, my second biennale. This time, I said to myself, I can't fuck up. But instead, I did it again. I filled the Italian pavilion with stuffed pigeons. I called them *Tourists* (1997). Venice, pigeons, tourists. Nothing could be more banal. To try to save face, I stuck some stolen bicycles in a corner. My second opportunity, squandered again.

I regrouped in Germany, where every ten years the small city of Münster hosts an exhibition of artworks in public places. I put the tower of animals in the city's museum, but

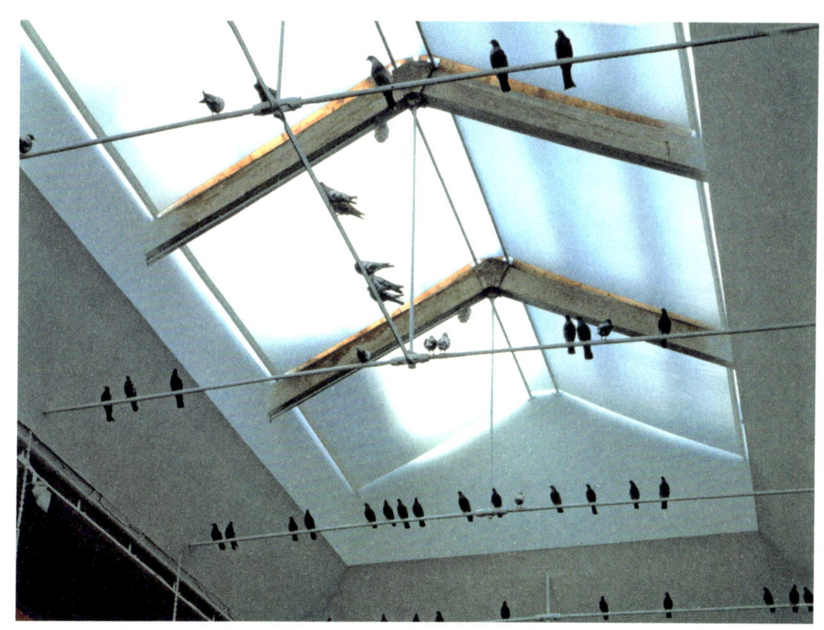

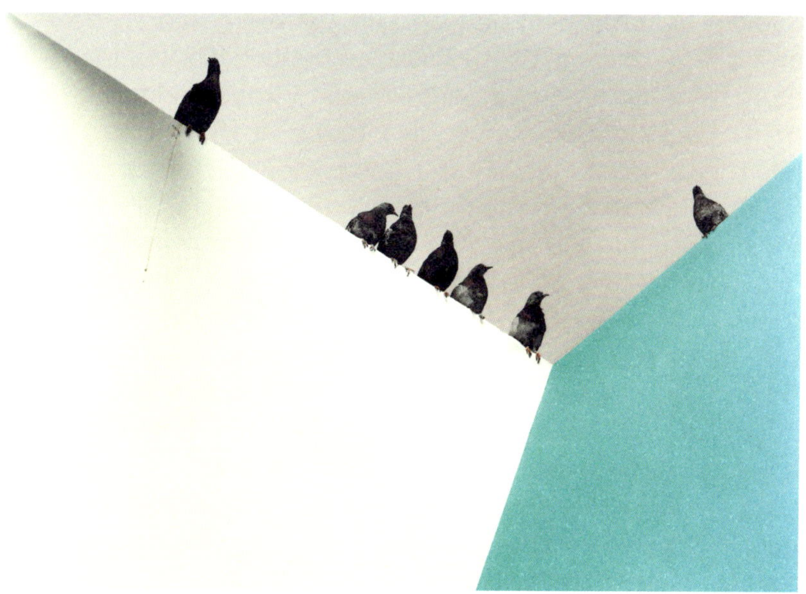

Installation view, *Tourists* (1997)
Biennale di Venezia, 1997

on this occasion I added the last chapter of the story to make *Love Lasts Forever* (1997). The same stacked animals, but now they had become skeletons. I've always been moved by the two figures in Pompeii, who died side by side. So I imagined myself and my friends, loving each other so much that we would become skeletons together, perhaps at a table in a restaurant. But then I used animals, because they forcefully conveyed the idea of someone who keeps on doing what he or she believes in, even after death. If someone has conviction, not even death can take that away. I have never wanted to be too dramatic in my works, or too direct. In short, these animals that bray, bark, mew, and crow are heroes for me, like the revolutionaries raising their arms in the famous painting by Goya. They do not raise their arms to surrender, but to rejoice, even when facing a firing squad. Just like these animals, who continue to sing their hymn of freedom.

My contribution to this exhibition did not end there. I also had to put something outdoors, in a public place. I rode around on a bicycle by the lake. Suddenly, or "out of the blue"—which then became the title of the work—I thought it might be fun to throw a corpse into the lake. It was all downhill from there. A week later, I was back with the dummy corpse. First thing in the morning I rented a boat and tossed the maiden into the lake. The work became something of an urban myth, a bit of hearsay. No one knows if I really threw the body into the lake. People visiting the exhibition would take boats and go searching for it. Some said they had seen something, others got mad because they saw nothing and felt cheated. Cattelan always pulls everyone's leg, they said. It was sort of like the Loch Ness Monster. Was it real or not?

I've always been interested in death and life. Both of them have always scared me. We spend our lives looking for love and we often try to hide from death. At times I use people to express what I want to say, but often animals speak of fear and suffering in a way that is different to that of humans. In Paris I put two sleeping dogs in a room at the Musée d'Art

Moderne de la Ville de Paris. They are dead, but they are still scary. First they scare you because they seem to be alive, but even afterwards, when you realize they are dead, you sense the presence of death and get scared. Even though they cannot hurt us, the dead are frightening. Having worked at the morgue, I must say that after a while you understand that the dead are objects and no longer people. When you see lots of them, you can no longer think of them as former living individuals. Life has really moved on, gone elsewhere. A dead body is a bit like an empty cage, lacking a canary. We know a bird used to be in there, and we wonder where it has gone. But the cage is still just a cage. The corpse is still just a corpse.

The year finally came to an end in New Mexico, and again I wound up working with a dead person: the American painter Georgia O'Keeffe. A new museum for her work was opening precisely when I was invited to the Santa Fe Biennial. They say there are spirits there of the Native American tribes that once lived and still live in the area. I played the wise guy with the spirit of the painter and had a mask of O'Keeffe made, like a carnival costume, or like those of Mickey Mouse and Goofy at Disneyland. During the opening, a person wore the big mask and walked around, and people could have their picture taken next to her, the way they do at Disneyland. When artists become famous they stop being people and become personalities, like in cartoons, no more and no less. While it is true that Mickey and Donald somehow exist, it is also true that when a human being becomes famous they no longer really exist, they become a character, someone fictional. Today I feel like Pluto, Mickey Mouse's dog, simultaneously real and fake. I've never understood why people get a kick out of having their picture on the wall standing next to a famous football player or an American president. I've always imagined a celebrity turning the situation around, and hanging pictures on his or her walls in which he or she is posing next to perfect nobodies, to remember that there is a real world of anonymous people out there, where folks breathe, eat, and defecate just like celebrities. I always wonder about that, when I see someone like President Obama. When does he go to the bathroom? I can imagine him saying "Excuse me, please," getting up, and disappearing for ten minutes. But even if I can imagine it, it all seems fake. In the end, Obama is like Mickey—someone who never has to relieve himself.

The experiment in New Mexico was a bit like the ones they did with the atom bomb. The experiments worked, but then to see if the bomb really worked they dropped it on people. I did the same thing. To see if this idea of the real person that becomes a fictional character really worked, if it had the right force to break into the art world and have an impact, the following year I dropped it on New York, in front of the Museum of Modern Art. Outside MoMA visitors found Picasso welcoming them and letting them have their picture taken with him. Picasso is perhaps the only artist who is as famous as Mickey Mouse, and MoMA is a bit like the Disneyland of modern art. The normal folks smiled and had fun, while inside the museum, the curators who had invited me were turning up their noses. They felt like they were being jeered at, because they think Picasso is a serious thing. I agree that Picasso is something serious, but so is Donald Duck. Donald brings in more people and more money than Picasso. I didn't manage to really hit the target. The art world swayed with the blow but remained standing. My attempt to break through reality with the fiction of art was only half a success. It was back to the drawing board.

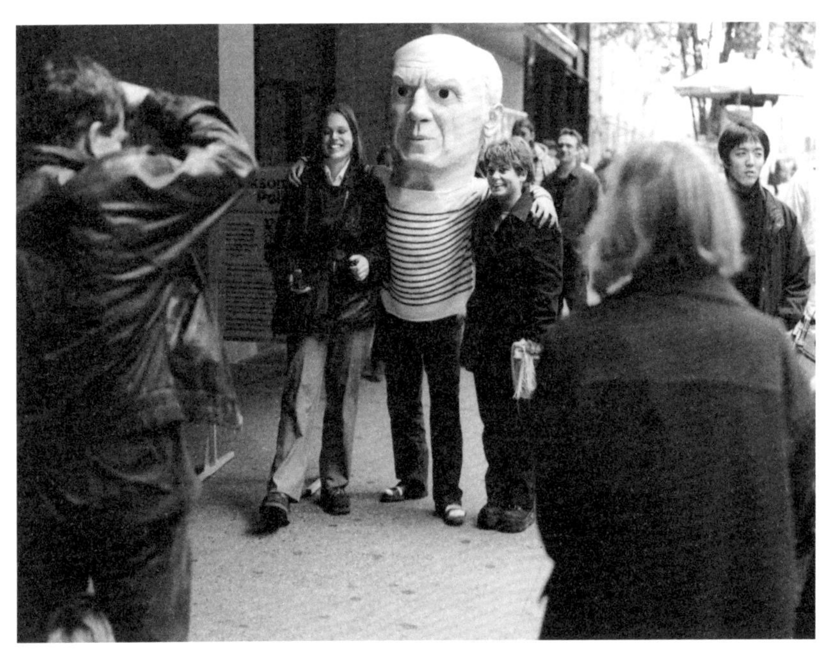

Untitled (1998) in
Projects 65: Maurizio Cattelan,
Museum of Modern Art, New York, 1998

Even Birds Can Bark

The fate of animals has always made me feel sad. Forced to be what they are for their entire lives. If humans can change identity, sex, jobs, husbands, and wives, the color of their hair, the shape of their nose, why do poor animals always have to remain as they are? I imagined a starling who wakes up and realizes there's a dog inside him. He can't do anything about it. No, the starling that realizes he's actually a dog has no options. Unless someone tries to help him. There's no harm in trying. So one day I bought a whole flock of mynah birds, the ones that learn how to imitate voices, and I took them to a friend's kennels where the dogs were always barking.

I left the birds there, in their cages, for many months, near the dogs. When I came back nearly all the birds had learned how to bark. Some did it better than others. I took a couple back home. For one year they were my watchdogs. When someone approached my door they would start to bark like mad, and scare the intruders away. Then, little by little, they forgot how to bark and began to speak Arabic, imitating my neighbors who shouted in the courtyard. I had to get rid of the birds because they would wake me up at night and I would think someone had entered the house and was talking to me in Arabic. I gave them to a Moroccan shopkeeper, who was very pleased. Every so often I drop by his shop, and one of the mynah birds is still there; the other one died, but the survivor speaks perfect Arabic. The whole thing was rather satisfying. I had managed to change an animal's identity and culture. The “Muezzin Mynah Bird,” one of my best works of art. I even thought about showing it in some museum or gallery, but then I decided it might be a mistake, and a bit racist. I would incur the wrath of animal rights advocates and fundamentalists, maybe even linguists.

Despite No Spite

They say my art is one of spite. It needs a target, to humiliate or embarrass someone. The day I run out of spite I'll have nothing else to say.

But that isn't really the case. Respect and disrespect always get mixed up in my mind. When I respect someone or something, I get the urge to somehow bring them into what I am doing. That might be a mistake. When I don't respect somebody, my instinct tells me to do something spiteful. I did that in an exhibition in London. I have never been able to stand soccer fans. Once, in Padua, a group of soccer diehards followed me and one of my friends, I can't remember why. Since then I have always hated them all, of all races, all teams, all nationalities. I got to London on a Saturday evening and ran straight into a group of hooligans on the way back from a match; they were blind drunk and it was impossible to tell if their team had won or lost—they were in terrible shape either way. The next morning, when I met with the gallerist who wanted to do the show, I told him my work would simply be a black granite slab with all the matches the English national team had lost engraved on it. He stared at me with the cold eyes and idiotic grin only the English can muster. I understood that he hated me but was too polite to say it. Two days after the opening we received death threats. I have never worked with that gallerist again, and I've seldom been invited back to England.

When I got back to Milan I told my gallerist friend about the English reaction. He told me that if I dared to do the same thing with all the matches lost by AC Milan, the team he supported, he'd pin me against the wall. I told him that was a great idea.

When the time came to do another show at his gallery, the work consisted precisely of the gallerist stuck to the wall with industrial tape. A real crucifixion. And one that almost worked. After a few hours, the poor sucker, pale as a corpse, raised his eyes to the heavens and said: "Maurizio, Maurizio, why have you forsaken me?" One hour later he was in an ambulance rushing to the emergency room—he had collapsed. Everyone thought we had planned the whole thing. But the truth was that the poor guy had really run the risk of kicking the bucket.

Fiction and reality are very mixed up in my work and my way of thinking. For many years I asked other people to answer questions for me in interviews, and sometimes I sent stand-ins to speak for me in public. Then it became a formula that didn't work anymore, so I braced myself and went it alone. At first it was a real trial. I'd return home after the event feeling exhausted and drained. I had done my worst. I looked at Pope John Paul II on television, who traveled all over the world in his heavy vestments, with Parkinson's Disease, tired, and elderly, but never failing to get the job done. I wondered how he did it, how he could make such a monstrous sacrifice. I would have died on the spot; I didn't even have the strength to chat up a tiny art world audience.

For me Wojtyla was something of a legend. I was invited to do a show in Basel where the director of the museum was Polish. "I'll give you a gift," I said. So I showed up with a sculpture of the pope holding his staff with the crucifix. I covered the room on the first floor of the museum with red carpet, and together with my faithful friend from Milan tried to install the statue of the pope so that it would stand up. But once it was standing, I realized it was horrible. The exhibition was going to open the next day, and we had no alternatives. We stayed in the museum all night trying to find a way out—a solution that just didn't want to come.

We dozed off and I dreamed about my father. I never remember my dreams, and what's more, I never dream about members of my family. That night, though, my father appeared to me in a dream. I don't recall ever seeing my father look tired, not even after very long days of work behind the wheel of his van. But in the dream he was exhausted, as if burdened by the fatigue of a whole life that had suddenly crept up on him. I woke up with a start. The pope was standing there, in front of me. I woke my friend and said: "We have to break his legs." He thought I had gone mad and didn't understand whose legs I was talking about: "The curator's?" "No, we have to break the pope's legs." So we took a saw and cut off the legs at the knees, and the poor guy collapsed to the floor, wasted. That still didn't do the trick, though. So we went out, found a stone quarry, and ordered a boulder.

There were only a few hours left before the opening. The museum director, who already looked like Dracula anyway, was as white as a sheet. When he saw the poor pope stretched out on the floor, he got even paler. He mumbled something. Then, when the truck unloaded the boulder and we had rolled it, with enormous effort, on top of the legs of his holiness, the unlucky bloke made a halfhearted attempt to stop us. After all, Wojtyla was the most famous Pole of all, and manhandling him like that might have had a very bad impact on the young director's career. But it was too late. To make matters worse, we broke the skylight in the room to make it look like the rock was a meteorite that had fallen from the sky, sent by God to stop this overly zealous servant—perhaps for his arrogant refusal to accept the weight and the infirmities of the flesh that ordered him to surrender.

"This will be the end of me," I thought, looking at the work. Instead, it was just the beginning. In Basel the work made

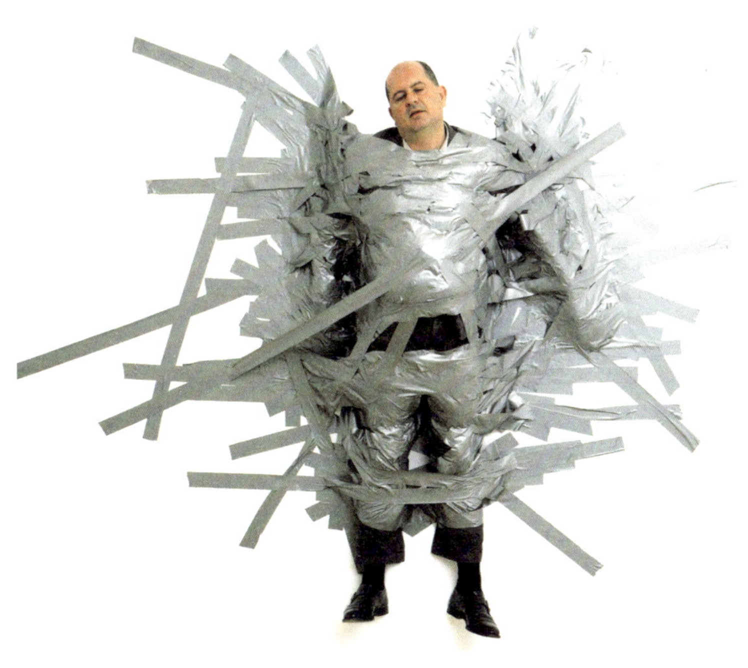

Installation view, *A Perfect Day*,
Massimo De Carlo, Milan, 1999

a little noise, but when I showed it in London, at the Royal Academy, the image of the crushed pope made its way around the world and ended up on the pages of all the newspapers. All of a sudden, finally, I was famous! It was a real physical sensation. I remember that I could feel, right inside me, inside my soul, that something had really and truly changed. I had broken the sound barrier. It was going to be very hard to reject me at this point. Not even the fakir buried alive at my third Biennale di Venezia had caused such a stir. I had found the right formula: the fame of the pope mixed with the feelings people had for him. Those who thought the success of the work was due to scandal, disrespect, or spite had it all wrong. The success of that sculpture, which will probably look dusty and dated in twenty years' time, came from the fact that I had managed—I don't know how—to give three-dimensional form to people's collective compassion for the pope. A contemporary act of mercy.

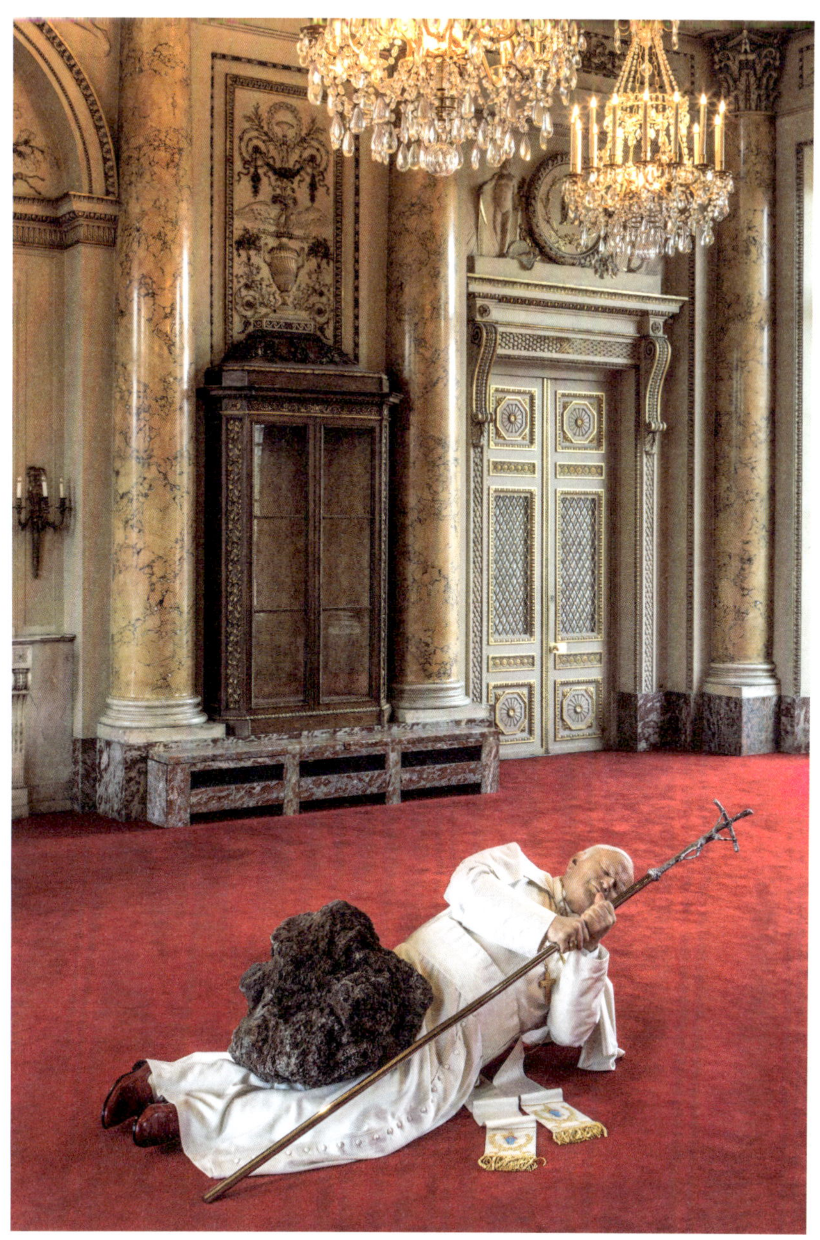

Installation view, *La Nona Ora* (1999) in *Not Afraid of Love*, Monnaie de Paris, 2016

The Ostrich Is Not a Chicken

Once I was so embarrassed to take part in an exhibition of Italian art that my work was a stuffed ostrich that was hiding its head in the wooden floor of the room. I've always felt like an ostrich. Never like a chicken.

Finally, though, I could pull out my head and take a deep breath. Although my body, my face, were becoming more famous than my works. "The pope? Yeah, it's by that guy with the big nose." You'd hear a lot of that. Someone told me I was becoming a sort of Joseph Beuys, the famous German artist, but homegrown. Beuys had made himself into an artwork. Criticism and malice have always stimulated me to create. So this rather backhanded Beuys compliment made me want to do a work about him. I talked it over with some people and we came up with lots of hypotheses: first to borrow his famous hat, then the fisherman's vest he always wore, then the overcoat with the wolf collar. Then I remembered the famous felt suit he had made and worn in one of his performances. But just wearing that suit would not be enough to make the thing work. It needed what one of my colleagues used to call "the surplus." For me the surplus was the scrap, the thing you set aside that sometimes worked better than the part you kept.

The felt suit got the nod. But something had to be done to it. Why not put it in the washing machine and see what happens? That was the first thing that came to mind. What could happen to a felt suit in a washing machine? It could shrink. Fine. But after the suit, you also get put in the machine, and you too emerge smaller. That was it. A shrunken self-portrait with a shrunken felt suit. The problem was what to do with the shrunken figure. Should it stand up? Sit? Lie down? No. When you take something out of the washing machine you hang it up to dry. So we hung my self-portrait up to dry on a coat rack that became the base of the sculpture.

The title? It was a tribute to Beuys: *La Rivoluzione siamo noi* (*We are the Revolution*) (2000). Also because I kind of believe the same thing myself. We make the revolution, not others. In Padua I had witnessed the revolution done by others, and in the end nothing happened. This time I wasn't planning to get shafted. I'd make my own revolution, or at least in the company of those I wanted to have along for the ride.

I showed my shrunken self in Zurich, in a totally empty space. People walked and walked until in the end they found this little man hung out to dry, who looked you in the eye, rather devilishly, as if he were thinking, "Fuck off, Beuys . . ."

Los Palermoles

Right on time, every two years, comes the Biennale di Venezia. This would be my fourth. I didn't feel much like another fiasco. But it would be impossible to cop out. At least for me—someone who says "yes" about twenty times for every "no" I can muster. I wanted to think it over carefully, though.

I went on vacation to Sicily. One day when I was driving around Palermo I looked up at the hills around the city, and they reminded me of the hills in Los Angeles. In fact, they were exactly the same. I went exploring, and found myself on top of a mountain of trash, an enormous dump run by the Mafia. Can the way you imagine a place change its reality? Los Angeles was not just the city of Hollywood, it was also the place of brutal murders, like the crimes of O.J. Simpson or Charles Manson, the city of race riots and earthquakes. Nevertheless, the big Hollywood sign always got the better of reality. Dreams die hard, unlike lies that contain the seeds of their own demise. So why not build a sign just like the one in Hollywood on one of these dumps in Palermo, to bring a bit of imagination to a world that seems to have little of the first and even less of the second? So I decided my work for the biennale would be the Hollywood sign, full size. A folly like that of Werner Herzog's *Fitzcarraldo* (1982). A real challenge, which I could afford after the success of the pope and the money that was coming in from sales of works. The idea that you could make people forget about violence for a few moments just by moving a symbol from one place to another

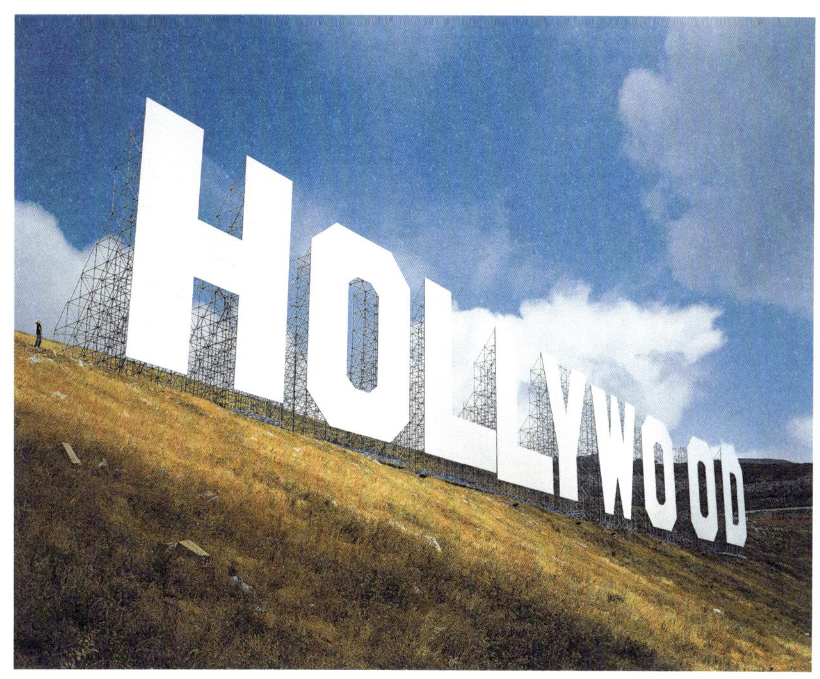

Installation view, *Hollywood* (2001), special project for the Biennale di Venezia, Palermo, Sicily, 2001

seemed like an experiment worth trying. It was worthy of risking time, money, and reputation to do something few people would perhaps see, but that would definitely be talked about by many.

When I saw the first letter of *Hollywood* (2001) looming against the sky, from down in the valley, even I felt confused, and for a moment I forgot where in the world I was. I hadn't moved the sign from Los Angeles to Palermo, I had actually moved Palermo to Los Angeles.

May Our Trespasses Forgive Us

Our sins are not to blame. If we didn't commit them, they wouldn't exist. Before asking God for forgiveness, we should ask it of our sins.

I was in Sweden, in the winter. Pitch black. Deep depression. I was going through not so much a spiritual as a vegetable crisis, given the total lack of fresh produce in the Swedish diet. Dark thoughts hovered in the air in the hotel room. I wondered if an artwork can be a means of redemption. If you can make a pile of horrible things, and then all of a sudden come up with a masterpiece. Would God accept one masterpiece as a means of redemption? Go figure.
I wondered: What if Hitler, after all the things he did, had turned out an exceptional work of art, on the same level as the Sistine Chapel, would the heavenly father have granted him at least a few indulgences? My answer was no. Art does not have such supernatural power. Art is made for men, God couldn't care less about art. I'm almost certain of that. When I die and go someplace else, God won't have the slightest idea about the difference between me, Bernini, and Caravaggio. No. Maybe art can save us on earth, but not in Heaven.

Hitler. I thought about Hitler. If I met someone with the face of Hitler in the street, but I didn't know anything about Hitler, would I think he had the face of a criminal? Who knows? We have the symbols and faces of evil and good so clearly imprinted in our minds that it is hard, even impossible, to

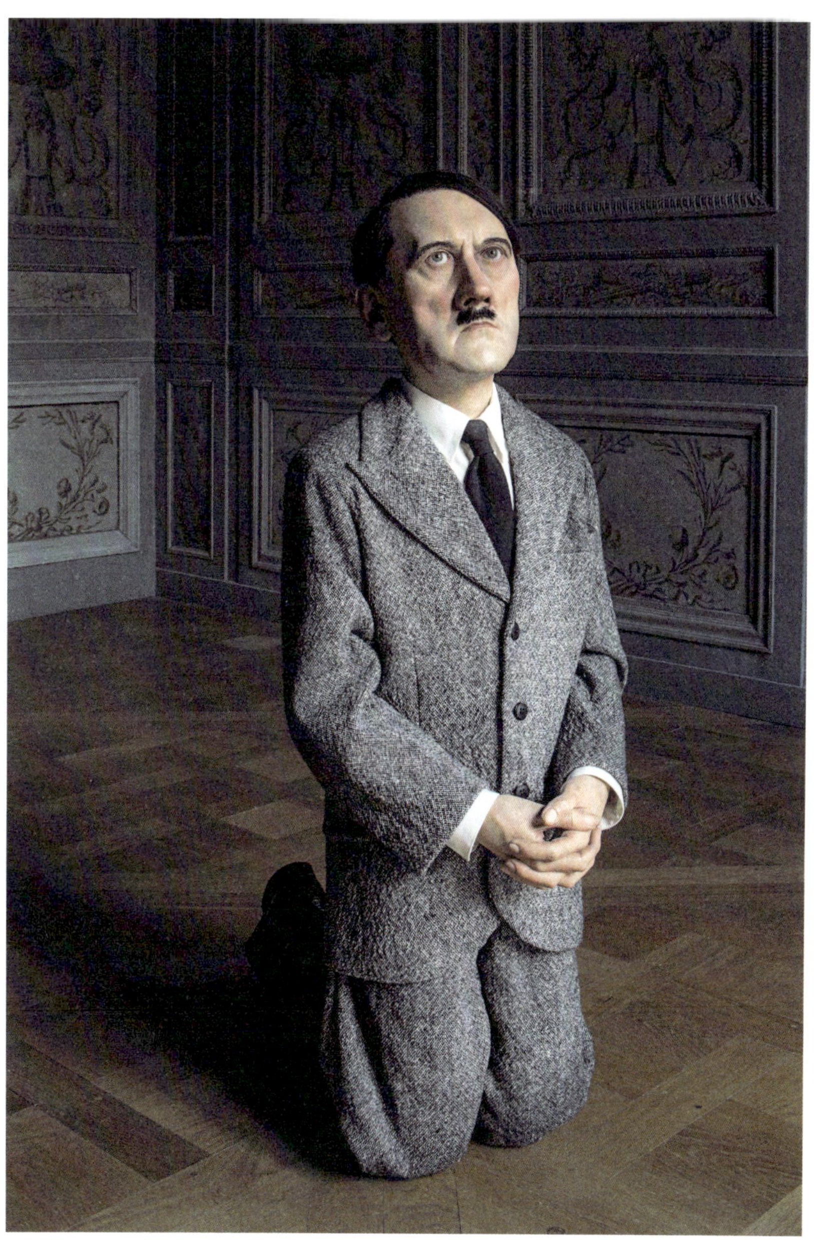

Installation view, *Him* (2001) in
***Not Afraid of Love*, Monnaie de Paris, 2016**

forget them. So from one red herring to the next, I got the idea for this sculpture in an immense space in Stockholm that seems like an industrial Gothic cathedral. At the back, the viewer sees this kneeling figure, praying. The closer you get, the better you can see that the person is not an adult, but a boy. Approaching him quietly from behind, so as not to disturb him, you move to one side to see the boy's face. Then you stop short—the figure is a miniature Hitler, with his eyes raised to heaven, praying. After the first shock comes a second impulse, and you feel tenderness for this butcher who is perhaps begging for forgiveness. But you can't do it. It is forbidden. Even though, when seen in this guise, he doesn't seem like a bad guy. This is the question I was wondering about, and wanted to pose to viewers with this work: Does evil have to seem nasty in order to scare us, to make us defend ourselves, and fight back?

I had already done some artistic experiments on the themes of violence and Nazism in the past. When I was invited to do a show in Germany I proposed plastering the whole town with posters announcing a skinhead rally on the same day as the opening, in the same town. I wanted the art world to have to come to terms with completely different, even opposite people. Evil vs. what we consider Good, namely Art. The proposal was rejected.

Now, with Hitler, I was trying to condense this idea in an absolute symbol of evil. Also thanks to a friend, I had called the work *Him* (2001). A title that for some mysterious reason left no room for doubt or other possible interpretations. It was Him, without question, and there could be no escape route for our consciousness and our thoughts.

The Endless Return to Madonna Street

I've never been able to stick to the same wavelength. After *Him* I needed to lower the temperature of my brain, my ideas, and get back in touch with myself, with that inner curiosity that external visibility erodes day after day. I wanted to go back to being the usual suspect. But success is an irreversible process. Which doesn't mean that you will always have success. It just means that success transforms you into a different person, and not even total failure can free you from its grip.

I was back in Holland, where they remembered me for the gallery heist. For them I was a thief, and a thief I would remain, though this time in a less realistic, more theatrical way. One day the guard of a museum in Rotterdam, entering one of its rooms, found a nice surprise: a hole in the floor and a strange figure, with my features, poking through it. The guard was amazed, a bit like Capannelle in *Big Deal on Madonna Street* when he sees his friends burst into the kitchen through the wall. The year 2001, from an artistic viewpoint, ended like that for me. Before September 11 came along and changed the rules of the game.

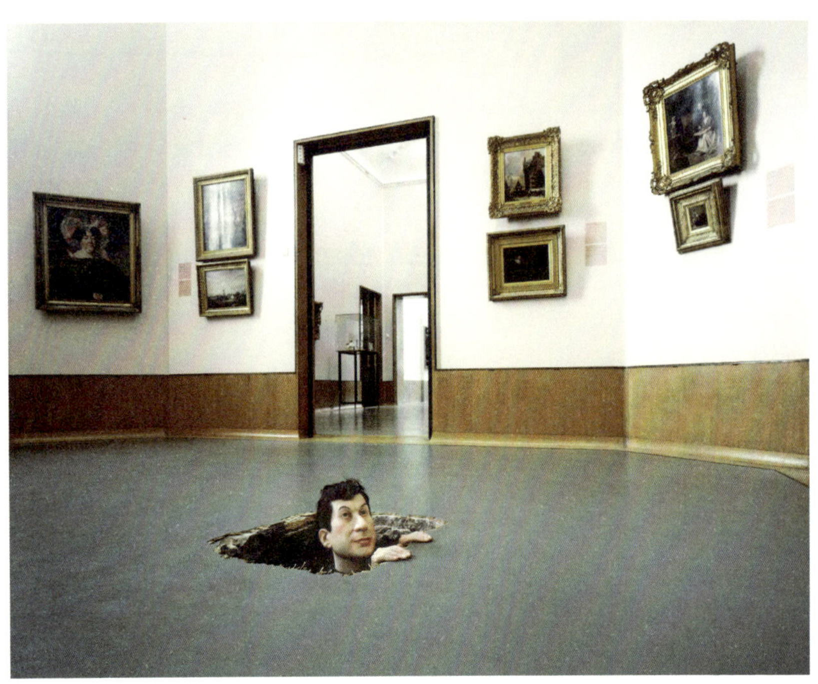

**Installation view, *Untitled* (2001)
Museum Boijmans Van Beuningen, Rotterdam,
Netherlands, 2001**

The World Upside-Down

The world can be enlarged, or shrunk, or turned upside down. These are the tricks of the artist who has run out of ideas, or never had any in the first place. I have tried all three of these methods, but I've had less success with enlargement. Once I enlarged the skeleton of a cat to make it look like a dinosaur, with rather disastrous results. Turning things upside down was another thing I hadn't explored much. I did it in a gallery show in New York: two policemen, upside-down.

After September 11, I felt like everything had been turned over. The poor cops were supposed to represent that. Power turned upside down by unpredictable events. They looked just like two normal police officers, but there was something very violent about the fact that they were upside-down. They reminded me of the bodies of Benito Mussolini and Claretta Petacci at Piazzale Loreto in Milan. Rough justice, in short—that of the police and also that of September 11. The world seemed to be based only on reckonings, vendetta, retaliation. Violence as an inescapable solution interested me a lot.

In Milan I lynched several children, dangling them from a tree in a public square. The reaction was only to be expected—predictable, banal. The work in itself was terrible, unbearable. But what I really wanted was to get on people's nerves. My question was: What is the difference between killing a child and killing an adult? I think there is no difference. Crimes are committed against humanity, not against generations. Faced with death we are all defenseless, just as we are when faced

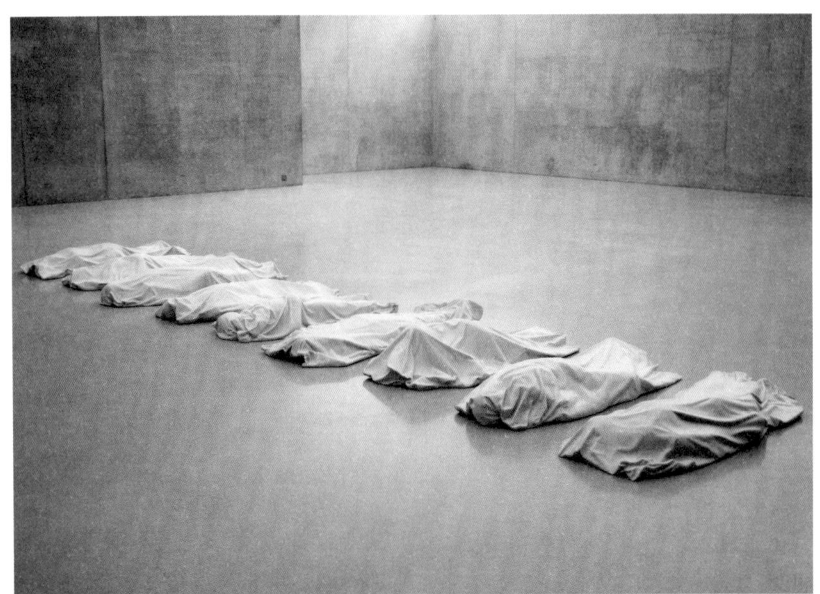

Installation view, *All* (2007)
Kunsthaus Bregenz, Austria, 2008

with violence. I have never understood the custom of granting preference to the elderly, to women and children, leaving behind middle-aged men and teenagers, as if they were equipped with better means to defend themselves from human madness. Death is not an airplane where some people have the right to priority boarding. This is why I called my nine corpses covered by a sheet *All* (2007). Once we bite the dust there are no distinctions. We're all the same. Identical. Things with no more function, no more fiscal entity for reckoning.

I have never found death, which I looked not so much in the face, as at the feet, when I was in the morgue, to be very likeable. Not because it forces us to finish that job half-done, known as life, but because it never tells us the truth. To find the truth I have tried to fake my own death, digging my grave, preparing gravestones for the cemetery. But it is all

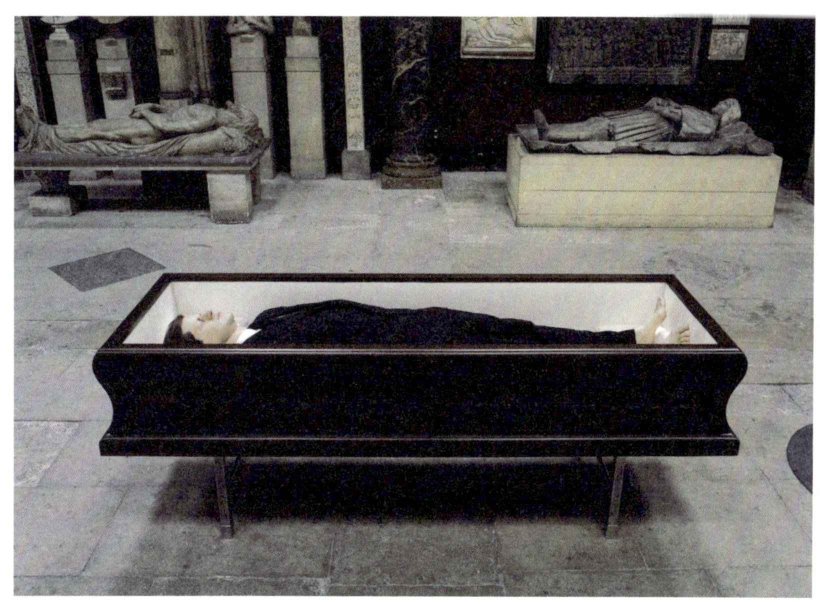

Installation view, *Now* (2004)
Chapelle des Petits Augustins, Beaux-Arts de Paris, 2004

useless, like getting ready for war in Texas when the war is in Iraq, with different people, in different places. Death is always and only now. That's the title of my dead JFK, without shoes and socks, in a coffin: *Now* (2004). Because certain deaths never end, they are eternal, they continue in the present, like that of Kennedy. Putting him in a coffin, for me, meant making him die once and for all, interrupting this cycle of hypotheses and eternal reincarnations in the news. I didn't have any special reason for removing his shoes and socks. I just think you shouldn't wear them in a coffin. It's like going to bed.

The Art of Luck

I have never played poker, but art is like poker. Lots of strategy, lots of bluffing, and a huge dose of luck. Clint Eastwood said the same thing, talking about his career and his success. There have been many moments when I was holding nothing, but I still called, and the others had less, so I was lucky. Like at my fifth Biennale di Venezia, where I sent out my umpteenth self-portrait, this time as a boy riding around on a tricycle. I never had a tricycle. I learned to ride a bike when I was ten, and I managed to buy my first bicycle when I was sixteen. For me, it was an artwork that allowed me to vanish when I wanted to, and to reappear at the right moment. This is the strategy I have tried to apply my whole life, though as the years passed the temptation to appear became stronger than the temptation to hide. The fear that nobody will come looking for you is still overwhelming.

One Sunday, as a child, I remember I hid in the house to scare my parents, but they just went to take a nap and I ended up in a closet for half an hour, until I fell asleep too. When I woke up, the house was empty. They were outside looking for me, worried and upset, while I was in the house, worried that they had abandoned me there. One of my uncles, as I said, either as a prank or to scare me, once told me that I wasn't really my parents' child, that I had been left near the house in a basket. I started crying and it took ages to convince me that it wasn't true.

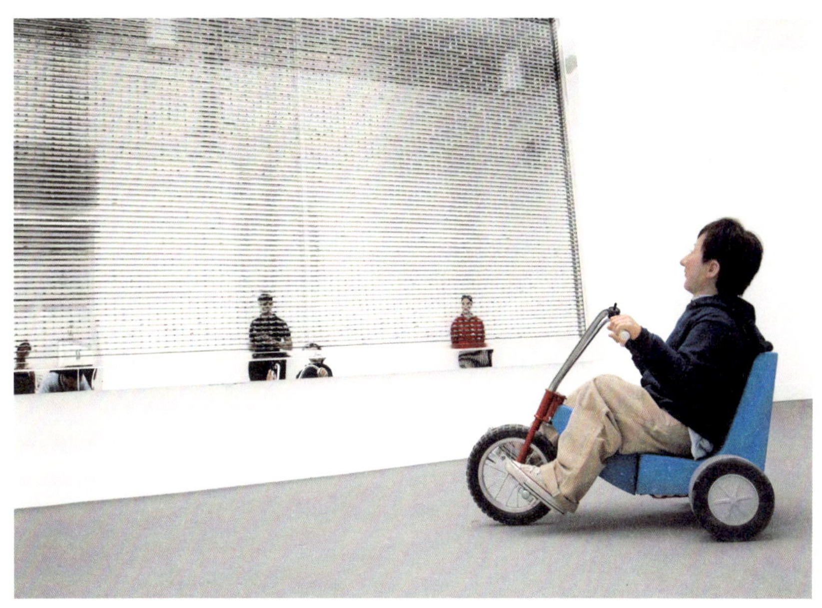

Installation view, *Charlie* (2003)
Biennale di Venezia, 2003

The doubt has always stayed with me. To hide, to be abandoned, to vanish, to escape have always been the temptations and the conflicts of my life. This way of coping with life has created big problems for me, especially with women. Somehow art has saved me, and it is the thing to which I have been faithful for the longest time. Over thirty years. My longest relationship has been with art. It has also been my most lasting work. It took me over ten years to convince myself that I was really an artist and that art was somehow convinced of the same thing and that it really loved me. After all, art has been the only thing for which I have betrayed. Otherwise I would have been a faithful person, to friends, women, gallerists. But nobody should ever ask me to abandon art. Art will decide when our relationship is no longer working; when the kitty of ideas is so small that the problem can no longer be overlooked.

The Man in the Bottle

The woman I have loved best was the one who won my heart and convinced me to go up to her place by offering me a salami sandwich at three in the morning. Not her body, just a sandwich. When I finished the sandwich, I tried to kiss her but she kicked me out and sent me home. Now that seduced me. When a man prefers a sandwich to kisses, like me, in the end he has a big problem. But I have always gone for the sandwich, over everything else. I have always had the ambition to change something in my life, but when all is said and done I've never really managed to do it. For me, art has been an enormous alibi, like the sick wife for guys who can never make up their mind to get a divorce and go and live with their lover. From the moment I looked into the mirror of that artist in the gallery in Padua, I don't think I have changed much. Even my body is pretty much the same. The same narrow waist, the same skinny legs. As if I had grown up with half my body inside a bottle, like the Genie of the Lamp.

I really did get the idea of hatching and raising a bird inside a bottle. As a kid, I had seen pears that grew inside bottles which were attached to the branches of trees, and were to be filled with grappa. I thought it was a miracle. At home we had two parakeets. One day they laid an egg and I took it on the sly, put it inside a milk bottle, and hid it under my bed. Every day I would check it, to see if the baby bird had hatched, but of course it never did. That was my first unwitting attempt to be an artist. But it was also my first disaster.

Ideas, in the end, are just eggs. Nothing hatches if we keep them shut up in the bottle of our head.

When I went on a school field trip for the first time, to an anatomy museum, and I saw those glass jars containing dead fetuses, I thought children were born inside jars. The idea of being born in a jar scared me witless. When my mother got pregnant with my first sister, I thought she had a jar inside her belly. My father, a man of few words, had a lot of trouble trying to explain to me that that was not the case. But the idea of being born like those pears inside a bottle has always fascinated me. Art, in the end, is a big bottle in which artists grow. They see the world through the glass, but they can never really be part of it. We are privileged but also excluded. A part of us wants the bottle to break, another part wants it to stay intact. Life is good inside the bottle.

To be born in a bottle. “They are sleeping,” the teacher would tell us as we stared at the fetuses with their closed eyes. I didn’t know that you can die before being born, but to me those children didn’t look like they were sleeping. For a while I had a lingering fear of being closed up inside a bottle. I would wake up crying and run to my parents, who would soothe me and put me back to bed. I could never have imagined that I would end up sticking myself inside the big bottle of art with people staring at me from the outside, the way I stared at the fetuses in the museum—a bit afraid, a bit repelled, somewhat in awe. I have tried everything to make sure they would look at me, and at what I have done, without fear and repulsion, but only with awe. I have almost never managed to do it. There are a lot more rotten eggs in my art career than little birds that have hatched healthy and strong. But I have been lucky that at least a few parakeets have hatched, and are now flying free.

There are a few, which I would have liked to catch again and put to sleep, but that’s OK too. Dogs, ostriches, rats, donkeys, pigeons, cows, and squirrels have sacrificed themselves in the name of my art, courageously, unquestioningly, without even knowing that their fate might be to become a masterpiece or, more often than not, a fiasco. If some animal has survived its fate as an artwork, may it enjoy its freedom. I would have done the same in its place. The biggest risk, in fact, for everyone, but especially for an artist, is to wind up becoming an artwork—to become what you do and not what you would like to be. When the ideas get weaker than the person who thought them up, a red warning light goes on. Red alert. Evacuate the zone! Abandon ship! Get out of the bottle before they cork it again.

Ascension and Liberation

The Solomon R. Guggenheim Museum in New York is like an upside-down Tower of Babel. The architect did not want to reach the sky, he wanted the artists who enter there to know hell. An artist who enters the spiral of this building loses all hope of getting out alive. Often, as happened with the Tower of Babel, you can no longer tell what was meant by anything. Physically and mentally, the space is a vortex that can only swallow you up and make you disappear. If you make the situation worse, as I did, by arriving a bit worn out and without ideas, there is really no escape. I have never really prayed in my whole life. When they kicked me out of our neighborhood parish, I swore I would never again say even one Hail Mary. I believe I have more or less kept my vow. And yet, inside the Guggenheim rotunda, I felt the need to pray. I don't know to whom, I don't know why. But I felt this need to ask forgiveness, from someone, for everything I have done and everything I have failed to do in my life, as an artist and as a human being.

I asked forgiveness for having made fun of Lucio Fontana's cuts by making a Z for Zorro on canvases, for having stolen the idea of the monument to agriculture from poor Alighiero e Boetti, and having planted an olive tree in a cube of earth in the middle of a museum. I asked forgiveness from the priest whose statues of St. Anthony I had ruined with a marker. I begged forgiveness of the poor stuffed animals, of the wheel of Bel Paese cheese devoured by mice. I asked forgiveness for showing up to accept an honorary degree, pretending I had had an accident. I begged myself for forgiveness for not having taken myself seriously enough. Forgiveness for all the ideas of others with which I have become, if not rich, at least affluent. Forgiveness from the women I have cheated on with art, those I have left for art, those I have loved like artworks.

So while I was praying for forgiveness with my eyes glistening a bit with those tears I had carried around in my pocket my whole life, I raised my eyes to Heaven. Standing in the middle of the spiral of the museum, which held me inside it like a great maternal womb—still a little seed that didn't know if it would be male or female—I looked up. There was nothing. Until, little by little, like the souls on Judgment Day or the saints during the Ascension, all the artworks I had made over the last twenty years and more began to rise into the air. All of them, in no particular order, without ranking, seemed to have lost their weight. Not my works, but their souls, were rising to heaven. They were redeemed of their original sin of being dead. Heavy, useless things—the offspring of the vanity and greed of the world of images to which they had been exiled. One, two, three, four, fifty, sixty, one hundred, maybe even more. Not even I remembered having made so many. They didn't fly, they rose as if cushioned by air or attracted by a celestial force of gravitation. They returned to the womb of the imagination, back to being ideas, sensations, sentiments, fears, concerns, disappointments, and satisfactions. Each of them took its place up there, a place that seemed to have been designated long ago, perhaps even before they were born, before they were cogitated or imagined. I expected to suddenly feel the upward thrust myself, to rise together with them. But it did not come. My feet remained firmly on the ground. Fastened to the floor. I did not feel heavy, but my stringy legs seemed like roots, firmly planted in the ground.

Then everything returned to normal. The empty museum. The curator, beside me, asked me what I was going to do.

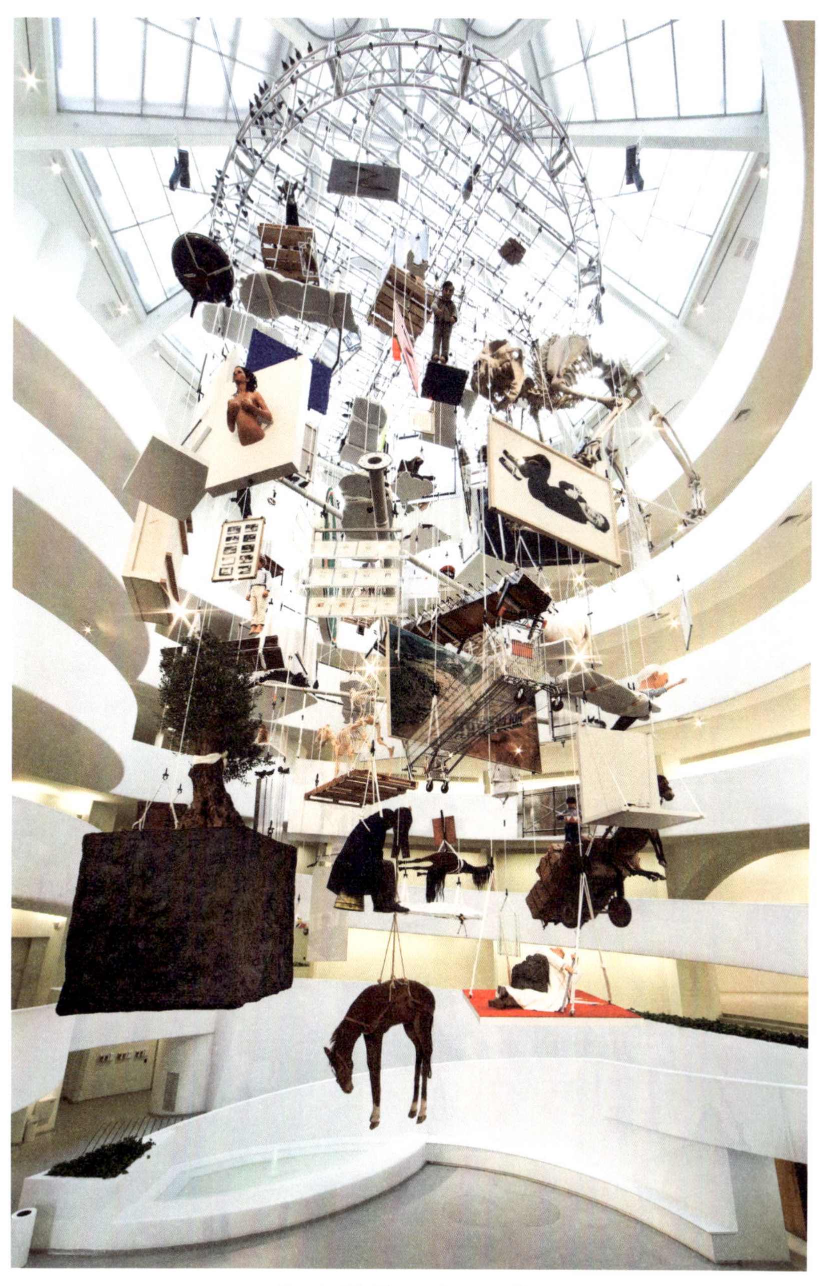

Installation view, *All*,
Solomon R. Guggenheim Museum, New York, 2011

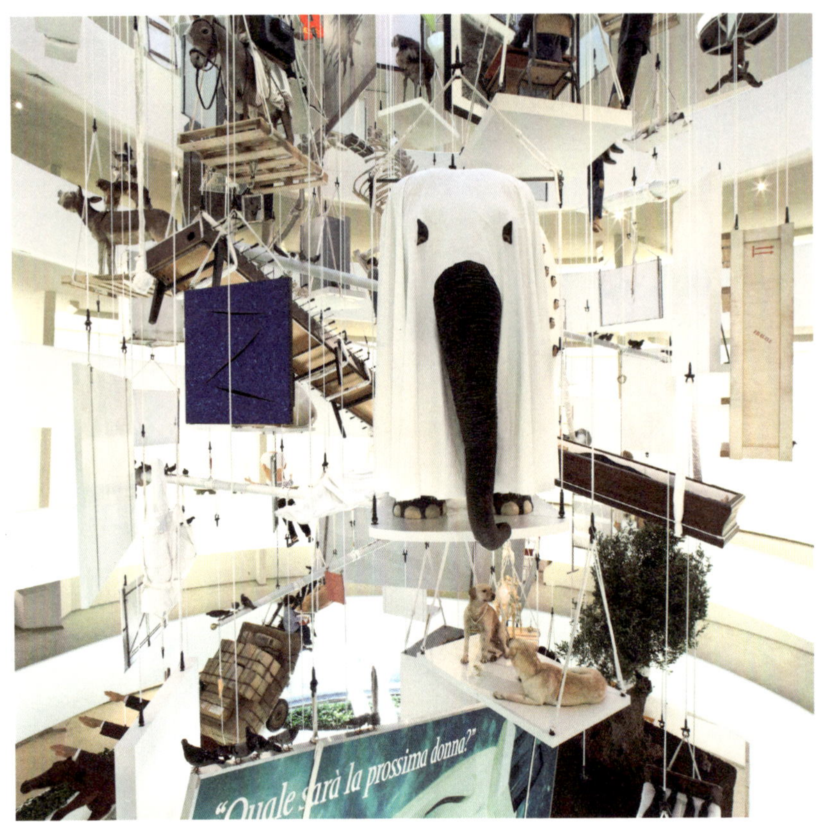

Installation view, *All*,
Solomon R. Guggenheim Museum, New York, 2011

What exhibition I would invent for her. Same old story, same old script—I had just seen the show: up there, suspended in the air. In the bottle now I saw the rest of the world in the form of a pear. I was down below, gazing up. I had nothing more to say. Nothing more to do. There was nothing left to decide. Nothing left to write. *Yes.*

Stuck! Yes! I am stuck.

Car and Mud

I felt as if my wheels were spinning in mud, until I realized I was in fact in mud. When you are in mud, the only thing you can do is wait for the rain to stop. It rained and rained some more. You think of the tears of that guy in *Blade Runner* (1982) running away in the rain. You are stuck. You cry. You are soaked with failure and success. It stinks. Maybe I was never an artist. Maybe artists do not exist—only people making stuff. Some are lucky and their stuff is called art. Some are unlucky and their stuff stays stuff no matter what. I think I was lucky, and yet, when I look back, a lot of my stuff was just stuff. When you are in mud, things sink inside you.

But eventually I dried out and those things popped up again; they are still stuff but they look like ancient stuff. The archeology of your own ideas. So, I chose to start dusting off what I found back there and work with it. The worst thing for any stuff is to turn old and never ancient. The fear of just looking old paralyzed me. You can be classic and still feel old but not ancient. Maybe the destiny of ideas is to only get old. Maybe that's the difference between art and ideas. One becomes ancient while the other just turns dusty, wrinkly, decrepit.

And where do my work and I stand? But then things happen. Shit happens and you don't care any longer about dust and wrinkles and you move out of your mud and you start again, acting like nothing happened, like everything is going to be OK.

Hanging on Love

When I was working at the morgue, once in a while you had to go and collect a dead body, wherever it was. Most of the time, if you had to pick up a body it meant that someone had killed him or herself. Once, I had to go and collect a guy who had hanged himself. The other mortician who was with me did not want to pull him down, so I had to climb up a ladder and free the poor fellow from the rope. When I was up there trying to untangle the noose, I looked at the guy's face, and his eyes were open, and it felt as if he were looking at me. It sounds gruesome but it wasn't. In fact, it was kind of reassuring. It was like he was telling me, "Hey, I just did what I had to do . . . I love her." I don't know if he killed himself for love but it looked like he did. His gaze stayed with me for a long time, and then I forgot about it.

My life is like a pig in a Chicago slaughter house: I use 99% of it. I don't throw anything away. The hanged man came back into my mind, and I started to fantasize about killing myself for love. Hanging myself for love. Where? In a bathroom. What would I wear? A dark suit, like for a wedding or funeral. So I did a self-portrait hanging. I titled it *YOU* (2021) because I killed myself for you. When it was finished, there it was, hanging in the studio. It was dead. Then I thought that if you hang yourself for love it is like the last date—the ultimate gesture in trying to conquer someone else. What do you do on say, the first date? You take some flowers. So you hang yourself, but you hold fresh flowers. I put a bunch of fresh colorful flowers in the hand of the guy—me—hanging, and he came to life. His eyes came alive, and I heard his words. I imagined him telling me, "Hey, I just did what I had to do . . . I love her . . . But, hey, don't worry . . . I love YOU."

Monument to Moment

The *Little Pissing Man* or *Manneken Pis*—the bronze child peeing in the faces of its audience in Brussels—has always been something of an obsession for me. The idea that a kid peeing is cute, while a grown up peeing is disgusting and offensive, annoys me immensely. I always wanted to make a monument of an adult peeing in public—to this moment of freedom, and defiance of unwritten societal rules. But when society forgets about you, you are allowed to forget about society. It was sometime in November, when walking around I don't remember where, I saw a guy kind of half asleep on a bench in a park pull out his dick and start peeing. He was the perfect model for the monument I wanted to create. As if the stupid boy in Brussels had grown up and ended up homeless, but was still peeing in public.

November is a strange month for me. It isn't fall nor is it winter. When I was a child, at the beginning of November, we didn't go to school on the Day of the Dead. Instead, I went to the cemetery with my parents to visit dead relatives and take them flowers. It was fun. While my parents were praying at the graves of their relatives, I ran around the graveyard and, when I was sure nobody could see me, I peed on the tombstone of some stranger. For that reason peeing outdoors, November, and death have always gone together for me.

When my friend Lucio died, I wanted to celebrate him before he entered, like everybody else, into the dusty archive of my memory. Lucio embodied a little bit of all the male figures in my life: friend, older brother, cousin, father, coach, advisor, consultant, assistant, sparring partner, alter ego. But in the end, I really don't know exactly who Lucio was for me. He hosted me when I was homeless and we talked a lot of this idea of peeing in public as a crime. I remember him laughing when I told him about peeing in an empty water bottle on a plane. So to celebrate him, I thought the best thing would be to make a monument of him half asleep on a bench, his dick in his hand, peeing on the floor. Maybe a floor of a museum, maybe the floor of a private collector's home. I wanted to celebrate the freedom we shared and a certain defiance of grown up rules we always shared. A monument to a lesser God of never-ending, liberating childlikeness.

Shitting and Shooting

Artists do things that haunt them forever. *America* (2016), the gold toilet, is one of those things.

The banality of shitting in gold or turning shit into gold. But the luxury of banality became gloomy and violent, or at least that's how it feels. When you shit, and you feel like shit, and everything looks like shit, then, I guess, the next step is shooting. You look outside the window and the landscape is shit, the food you eat is shit; you look in the mirror, and you look like shit. You start confusing life with shit and you start looking at the fame of shitty people and you just change two letters in the word "shitting" and you have "shooting." In your shitty head, shooting becomes the solution—not to a problem, but to an endless nothing. I always liked the final scene of Sam Peckinpah's *The Wild Bunch* (1969) when everybody is shooting everybody else. You can't understand who's shooting who. It was some kind of final judgment. And I remember when I saw *The Last Judgment* (1536–41) in the Sistine Chapel I could not figure out who was judging who—who were the baddies, and who were the goodies. So, for me, the closest thing to Michelangelo's *Judgment* is the ending to Peckinpah's film. That's how I think the last judgment will be, if indeed there is one. So I imagined a golden wall where people start shooting like crazy—for fun, for hate, for whatever reason they like, for revenge, for justice—who cares. *Jacio Ergo Sum*: I shoot, therefore I am.

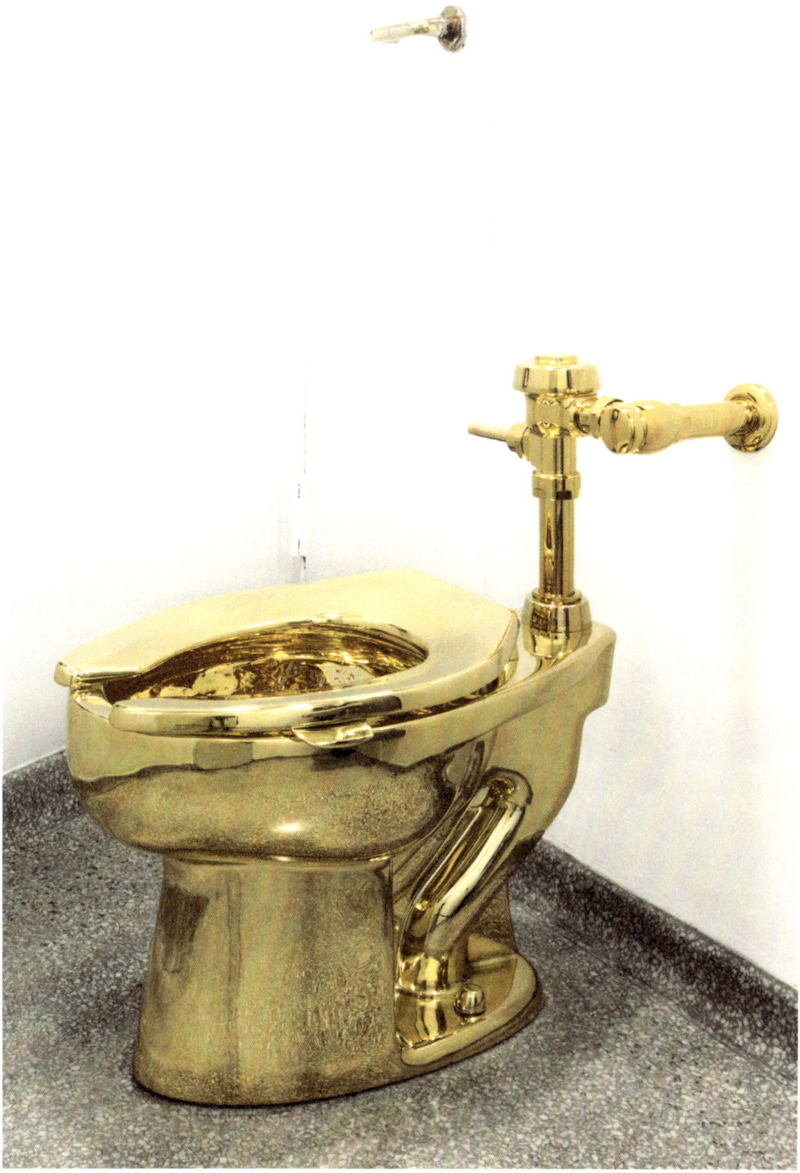

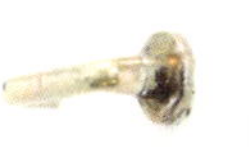

Installation view, *America* (2016)
Solomon R. Guggenheim Museum, New York, 2016

Crescent Banana

A banana is a crescent moon or a crescent moon is a banana. If you look at a banana, or at a crescent moon, you know what you are looking at. And when you know what you are looking at, that is the only time that doubt has abandoned you. For an artist, it is a moment of revelation. That's it!

In the Bible, the crescent is a symbol of rebirth and fertility. The mystery of the moon: *Mysterium lunae*. For me it was "Mysterium Bananae." If a mystery is stuck on a wall, it becomes a work of art. If the mystery is also a familiar mystery, like a banana, then maybe you have something that goes beyond art: above or below. A comedian's success is about revealing the mystery of humor within daily life. The comedian makes everything fun and profound at the same time—the audience laughs and experiences a moment of revelation. Yet the comedian is stuck with his or her own revelation until there is a new one. There is something tragic in any revelation and in any banana or any crescent moon. We know what it is. We are happy to know what it is. We are waiting for something else to appear with the same clarity. We are suspended in an endless waiting mode without the "force quit" command.

Crypto Stuck

I saw the banana and knew I wanted it to be a work of art. I just had to find the way to stick it on the wall. Once I found the way, I got stuck myself. I created a hidden or secret new way of communicating without knowing I was doing so. I invented an alternative reality from which I excluded myself or for which I don't know the password or the code needed to enter. It's like a party I organized in a home I own, but I don't have the keys to open the door, and outside a crowd of people is asking to enter. Nothing can convince them that I have another home where we can go and have the party, where the door is open. I locked myself out of my own art.

I need another planet. I need another form of life from where another form of art can help me to unlock and unstick myself.

Help!

The noise surrounding Maurizio Cattelan is underrated.

FINE.

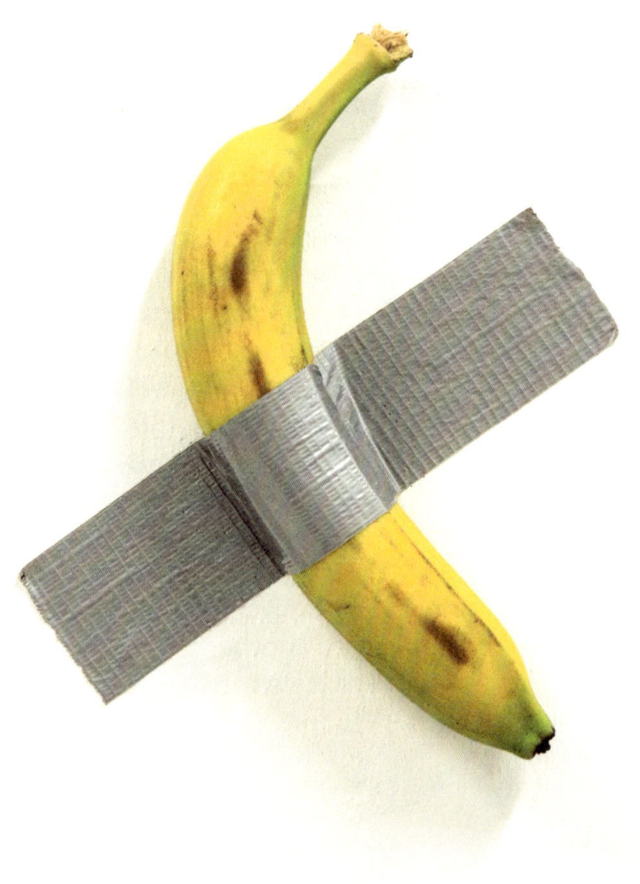

Comedian (2019)

Postscript

Yes. This book claims to talk about me. It insists on it. It makes me say things against my will. It has decided to be "Cattelan's Conscience," using a system that has none. Any reference to me is purely coincidental, as is any reference to persons or facts purported to have been around me or happened to me.

This book has been constructed with recollections and memories I had forgotten myself. A book full of mistakes that turn out, by chance, to be exactly right. I could sue the author.

Instead, I have decided to block its non-publication and to have the author sue me. Because if this book exists it is my fault, simply for existing. If I did not exist, neither would this book.

If I didn't want there to be a book about me, I should have thought about that sooner. The author is my victim, I forced him to get to know me. The harm done is the harm I have done to him. Take care not to raise doubts about what he says, but be cautious about believing even one single word of what he has written. This book demonstrates that truth is falsehood and lies have bowed legs. *Santa Bugia*, Saint Falsehood—the saint who holds a plate with a dunce's balls on top, one each representing me and the author.

Maurizio Cattelan

Stuck
Maurizio Cattelan: The Unauthorized Autobiography

980 Madison Avenue, New York, NY 10075

Senior director: Andisheh Avini
Chief creative officer: Alison McDonald
Director, publications: Brett Garde
Editor: Sara Harrison
Print production manager: Shiori Kawasaki
Project coordinators: Sloane Cameron and Chandler Sterling
Publication coordinators: Priya Bhatnagar, Lauren Mahony, Helen Redmond, Alexandra Samaras, and Rita Yirui Wang

Design by Philipp Hubert, New York
Color separations and printed by Pureprint Group, Uckfield, England

Cover drawing by Francesco Bonami

All photography courtesy Maurizio Cattelan Archive. Credits: pp. 32, 81, 99, 105, 113, 119, 120, and 130: Zeno Zotti; p. 51: STUDIO BLU–Giulio Buono; p. 61: Santi Caleca; p. 66: Marc Domage; p. 73: Lina Bertucci; p. 87 (top and bottom), 103, and 108: Attilio Maranzano; p. 91: Thomas Griesel; p. 97: Armin Linke; p. 110: Markus Tretter; p. 111: André Morin; and p. 127: Jacopo Zotti.

First published in Italian as *Maurizio Cattelan – Autobiografia non autorizzata* in 2011 and in English in 2013 by Mondadori and translated by Steve Piccolo.

This expanded edition features a new foreword and six additional chapters.

Gagosian would like to extend thanks to the author and the artist on the occasion of this new edition of the publication. We are grateful to Zeno Zotti and Jacopo Zotti of Maurizio Cattelan Archive for their support of this project.

Distributed by Rizzoli International Publications
300 Park Avenue South, New York, NY 10010
www.rizzoliusa.com

ISBN 978-1-951449-88-9
Library of Congress Control Number: 2025932835